Cooking for
CAREFREE
WEEKENDS

———

Molly Finn and Jeri Laber

SIMON AND SCHUSTER · NEW YORK

FOR
AUSTIN AND JIM
WITH LOVE

Contents

Contents

Menus for March, 46–47

Menus for April, 60–61

Contents

Menus for May, 78–79

Menus for June, 98–99

Menus for July, 112–113

Contents

Menus for August, 124–125

Menus for September, 136–137

Contents

Menus for October, 150–151

Menus for November, 164–165

Contents

Menus for December, 178–179

Foreword

Cooking for Carefree Weekends is for people who like cooking and good food, who enjoy having friends for the weekend but don't want to spend lonely hours working in the kitchen while everyone else is relaxing and having fun.

It's not easy to turn out a succession of splendid meals for weekend guests and make it all seem artless and effortless. It takes a particular kind of planning and a special approach to cooking—both of which we've worked out in the country homes where we spend weekends with our families and our friends. Unwilling to lower our standards by using the convenience foods that many people depend on, we have used our ingenuity instead to find ways to save time and simplify weekend cooking.

This book contains coordinated menus for twelve weekends, one for each month of the year. It tells you *when* to cook to avoid a lot of last-minute preparation, *how* to plan so that everything will be used (and used up) by Sunday night and *what* to serve in a series of simple, elegant meals, appropriate to both the season and the occasion.

Read the Weekend Menu a few days ahead so you'll have time to plan and get your marketing done. The Preparation Schedule that precedes each weekend's recipes will help you organize your work. It tells you which part of the cooking should be done before the weekend begins. Most of the dishes in this book can be prepared at least partially in advance. Many can be completed and then refrigerated or frozen. The few that require last-minute cooking are very easy to prepare. Cooking in advance makes sense whenever you entertain because you can do it at your own convenience and will then be free to be with your guests.

You can often prepare more than one meal at a time by cooking extra quantities of certain foods that can later be used as ingredients in new and entirely different dishes. You may have to hang a sign on the food you're saving saying "Hands off! For Sunday's lunch," but on Sunday you'll be glad that you did. Don't think of this extra food as "leftovers"; leftovers are often skimpy amounts of whatever happens to remain after a big dinner, and most recipes for leftovers are vain attempts to make them palatable. These recipes are all for dishes that are well worth making from scratch—whenever you cook for two meals at once, both meals will be equally good.

Although it won't really matter much to people who invite guests to their city or suburban homes, those who entertain in a weekend home want to be sure that all the food is gone by Sunday evening. In our menus we try to take into account the food that might otherwise be left behind in the refrigerator—the other half of the pineapple, for example, or those ubiquitous egg whites that are the by-product of many of our favorite recipes.

The amount of work varies considerably from weekend to weekend. Although there's always a balance between simple and complicated recipes, some menus—those for October, for example—call for especially little cooking while others, like the menus for our Russian weekend in April, demand a great deal of cooking in advance. Some dishes take a lot of time to make properly, but we include them because we think they're worth the trouble. If you try to simplify these recipes by substituting commercially prepared ingredients for fresh ones, they just won't taste as good. We try to avoid using a lot of canned foods; that may be the easiest way to cook, but it is certainly the least interesting. Only when we are convinced that it really *doesn't* make a difference do we indicate that canned or frozen foods are acceptable.

Our menus are designed to make the most of what each season offers; sometimes we've planned whole meals around vegetables. When fresh fruits and vegetables are in season they are abundant and cheap and usually suit the weather. Either raw or very simply cooked, they bear no resemblance to canned or frozen ones. Tomatoes are so good in September that we include them in four different meals that weekend. Certain fresh vegetables—turnips, carrots, cabbage, cauliflower, escarole and many others—are easy to get in winter, and they are the ones we use in our winter menus.

We have pared the menus down to essentials. There's usually lots of one or two good things in a meal, rather than a number of different courses. In many weekends, one food is used in two different ways or even the same way twice when we feel it's appropriate. When a soup or salad is especially good, we've made the most of it by using it as a main course. These weekend menus seldom include a first course; we find there's plenty to eat without it.

We've found other ways to simplify weekend cooking. We never serve fancy hors d'oeuvres with drinks. On the rare occasions when we serve anything at all, we use foods that don't need any preparation—nuts, olives, cherry tomatoes, cheese. We don't fix separate meals for children, though there's always a supply of hot dogs, tuna fish and peanut butter on hand for the finicky eater who just won't touch unfamiliar foods. Breakfast is usually a do-it-yourself affair.

All of our recipes serve six, except for the occasional layer cake which, of course, will go further.

Cooking for Carefree Weekends is designed for weekend hosts, but it will also be useful to anyone who does a lot of cooking and entertaining. It illustrates a way of planning and coordinating cooking which need not be abandoned on Sunday afternoon, and it contains many recipes for delicious, fresh and unpretentious food. We hope you will want to use these recipes again and again, not only on weekends and not only for guests.

Substitute Something Good

Obviously, there will be weekends when you don't have the time or energy to follow our menus to the letter. However, you can still use them, since there are ways to simplify them without changing their character too much.

Substitute something good that does *not* need preparation for something good that does. If you don't feel like fixing a dessert, for example, save it for another time and use fresh fruit or ice cream instead. Raw salads of various kinds can substitute for cooked vegetables if you find them easier to prepare. Or, if vegetables are particularly good and plentiful, leave out the meat!

You can skip cooking a meal altogether. Really good bread can be the basis of a delicious lunch or informal supper with nothing more added than an assortment of cheeses and jams, some sliced ham or some canned fish. Some of the lunches in this book require no cooking at all—Tossed Tuna Salad, Sardines, Cottage Cheese Lunch, Aioli Lunch, etc. Use one of them any weekend that's convenient.

In other words, keep the quality of the food high. Don't simplify by using quick but inferior versions of the recipes we've given; substitute something that's good in itself and doesn't need cooking.

Quantities

All of our recipes have been planned to serve six people, but they can easily be increased without any loss of quality. We hope that using these recipes will make entertaining such fun that you'll be doubling—or tripling—them frequently.

The Do-It-Yourself Breakfast

Because breakfast habits vary so much from family to family, we have learned to be flexible and take the cues from our guests. Not everyone wants to eat as soon as he gets up and not everyone gets up at the same time, especially on weekends. We sometimes like to sleep late on weekends, too, or to spend the early morning hours gardening or getting a head start on our cooking for the rest of the day.

We often use a do-it-yourself approach to breakfast. Young children—the earliest risers—can easily help themselves to cereal and milk if they know where to find them. A breakfast buffet set out on the kitchen counter might include oranges, bread, butter, marmalade, fruit, cheeses, doughnuts, coffee cake and lots of coffee. Add any appropriate goodies left in the refrigerator from the day before. Have some bacon and eggs available for those who want to fix them. People seem to like to help themselves.

If you want to serve a more formal breakfast and are looking for something a bit unusual, try one of the following recipes from this book:

Sausage Yorkshire Pudding, p. 171
Spoon Bread, p. 183
Omelette Provençale, p. 192
Corned Beef Home Fries and Eggs, p. 58
Coffee Cake, p. 59
Blini, p. 76
Kisselitza, p. 104
Clafoutis, p. 123
Cottage Cheese Pancakes, p. 156
Grilled Cream Cheese Sandwiches, p. 38
Zucchini Hash, p. 192
Prunes Crème Fraîche, p. 193

Menus for
JANUARY

FRIDAY DINNER

Baked Beef and Vegetables
Rice

•

Pot-Cheese Cake

SATURDAY LUNCH

Saturday Meat Salad
Italian Bread

·

Dried Fruits and Nuts

SATURDAY DINNER

Braised Ham
Home-Baked Beans
Hot Rolls
Cinnamon Applesauce
Assorted Raw Vegetables

·

Apricot Fool

SUNDAY LUNCH

Ham and Endive Mornay
Green Salad

·

Pot-Cheese Cake and Berries

Preparation Schedule

for

JANUARY

[ALL RECIPES SERVE 6]

Some of our weekend menus require advance cooking; others don't. Most allow some leeway, depending upon whether you want to do your cooking before or during the weekend.

This weekend's menus call for a particularly pleasant kind of winter cooking: something will be baking or simmering most of the time, filling the kitchen with good smells and demanding very little attention from the cook.

In Advance—A few of the dishes should be made in advance. Make the puree for the *Apricot Fool* as far in advance as you wish—it will keep indefinitely in the refrigerator. Bake the *Pot-Cheese Cake* on Thursday if you can, and prepare the *Cinnamon Applesauce*, too, if you don't have any in your freezer. You can get the *Baked Beef and Vegetables* for Friday all ready for the oven as much as a day in advance.

On Friday—Cook the beef early in the day on Friday or just before dinner if that's more convenient. The beans for Saturday's dinner have to soak overnight; don't forget to put them in water on Friday.

On Saturday—On Saturday morning, get the beans ready and put them in to bake no later than noon. Prepare the lunch, *Saturday Meat Salad*, using the cooked meat and rice in your refrigerator.

Braise the *Ham* whenever it's convenient during the day; if it cools, you can reheat it in the oven. Be sure to save the ham stock to use in the *Mornay Sauce* on Sunday and carve some extra ham at dinner for Sunday's lunch.

19

On Sunday—On Sunday, fix the salad and the *Mornay Sauce* while the endives are braising. You can assemble the *Ham and Endive Mornay* a few hours in advance and heat it in the oven just before serving. Slice the rest of the cheese cake, arrange it on a platter and garnish with strawberries.

FRIDAY DINNER

Baked Beef and Vegetables
Rice

·

Pot-Cheese Cake

BAKED BEEF AND VEGETABLES

We find that this dish—simple to make and an old family favorite—is also a perfect Friday night dinner for week-end guests.

> juice of 2 large lemons (4–6 tablespoons)
> 1 large clove garlic, minced
> lots of salt and freshly ground pepper
> 4–5 pounds beef for pot roast, preferably a 2-inch-thick
>   slice of boneless chuck, shoulder or round steak
>   (see note)
> 2 large Bermuda onions, peeled and thickly sliced
> 4 green peppers, seeded and sliced
> 1 eggplant, thinly sliced
> 1½ cups chili sauce

Preheat the oven to 325° F.

Mix half the lemon juice, the garlic and a generous sprinkling of salt and pepper in a large, flat roasting pan. Trim any fat from the meat. Season the meat by turning it in the pan and rubbing the lemon juice mixture in well. Put half the onion and pepper slices on top of the meat and arrange the eggplant and the remaining peppers and onions around it.

Combine the chili sauce with the rest of the lemon juice and more salt and pepper and pour it over the meat and vegetables. Cover the pan tightly with foil. Bake for 1½ hours. Serve the meat, sliced, on a platter and the vegetables and juices in a deep bowl.

If you prepare this dish in advance, slice the meat before reheating it.

NOTE—*Cook 2 extra pounds of meat if you intend to make Saturday Meat Salad, p. 23.*

RICE

Using your usual method, cook 2 cups of rice to serve with the Baked Beef. If you plan to make Saturday Meat Salad, p. 23, cook 4 cups of rice and set half of it aside.

POT-CHEESE CAKE

This large cake is ideal for weekends because it's just as good the second time you serve it. It is a splendid dessert, equally popular with adults, children and those who are "not especially fond of cheese cake."

CRUST

1½ *cups graham cracker crumbs*
 3 *tablespoons melted butter*
½ *cup sugar* } *mixed together*
 2 *teaspoons cinnamon*

FILLING

2 pounds pot cheese
1½ cups sugar
6 eggs, separated
juice of ½ lemon
1 cup heavy cream
½ cup cornstarch
½ teaspoon salt

fresh strawberries (for Sunday garnish)

Preheat the oven to 350° F.

Butter a 10-inch springform pan or a 9- by 13-inch baking pan, and press two-thirds of the crumb mixture against the sides and bottom.

Put the cheese in a very large mixing bowl, beat it for a minute or two and gradually add the sugar, egg yolks, lemon juice, cream, cornstarch and salt, mixing in each ingredient thoroughly before adding the next. Beat the egg whites until stiff but not dry and lightly fold them into the cheese mixture. Pour the batter into the pan, and sprinkle the remaining crumbs on top. Bake for one hour without opening the oven door; turn off the heat and leave the cake in the closed oven for another hour. Chill well before serving.

This cake can be safely transported in its pan in cool weather. Don't be afraid to make it in advance; it is even better after a day in the refrigerator. If a springform is used, remove the sides just before serving.

SATURDAY LUNCH

Saturday Meat Salad
Italian Bread

•

Dried Fruits and Nuts

SATURDAY MEAT SALAD

Although we invented this salad with the remainder of Friday night's Baked Beef in mind, it has been such a hit that we now find ourselves preparing Baked Beef with this meat salad in mind!

4 cups cooked pot roast or roast beef, cut into bite-sized pieces
6 cups cooked rice (2 cups uncooked)
4 scallions, including green tops, sliced
1 large green pepper, seeded and cut into bite-sized pieces
2 tomatoes, sliced in thin wedges, or 15 cherry tomatoes, sliced in half

DRESSING

2 tablespoons parsley, chopped
1 teaspoon fresh basil, chopped, or ½ teaspoon dried marjoram
2 cloves garlic, minced   ⎫
1½ teaspoons salt   ⎬ mixed together
lots of freshly ground pepper
½ cup olive oil
½ cup wine vinegar   ⎭

Combine the meat, rice, scallions, green pepper and tomatoes in a large serving bowl. Add the dressing and toss well.

This salad will keep for several days in the refrigerator and seems to improve with age.

DRIED FRUITS AND NUTS

A supply of dried fruits and nuts is an indispensable part of the weekend larder. Good in any combination, they make a simple and interesting dessert you can always have on hand.

A basket of nuts in their shells and a bowl of mixed dried apricots, figs, apples, cherries and prunes is an invitation to sit and relax, talk and nibble. A bowl of salted peanuts mixed with raisins is a good dessert in a pinch and one of the best snacks we know. Or, for a dessert as elegant as any, try a cluster of dried muscat grapes surrounded by shelled almonds.

SATURDAY DINNER

Braised Ham
Home-Baked Beans
Hot Rolls
Cinnamon Applesauce
Assorted Raw Vegetables

•

Apricot Fool

BRAISED HAM

Smoked ham takes on a distinctive flavor when it is cooked in this somewhat unusual manner, and it produces a rich stock which can be used in many wonderful ways.

2 *carrots*
2 *stalks celery* } *cut in chunks*
2 *onions, peeled*
3 *bay leaves*
6 *peppercorns*
2 *cups dry white wine*

2 *cans chicken broth* (*about 3 cups*)
½ *smoked ham, 6–8 pounds, or a 5-pound boned, canned*
   ham (see note)

Place the cut-up vegetables, seasonings, wine and broth in a large pot. Add the ham, bring the liquid to a boil, cover the pot tightly and simmer *very slowly* over low heat for about 2 hours, turning once if possible. If you do not have a large enough pot, you can cook the ham in a 300° F. oven, using a roasting pan tightly covered with foil.

Take the ham out of the pot. Slice it and arrange it on a platter. If you plan to carve the ham at the table, brown it first in a 425° F. oven after removing the rind and covering the fat generously with bread crumbs dotted with butter.

[Strain the ham stock and set aside one cup of it for Ham and Endive Mornay, p. 27. The rest of the stock should be frozen or used to make Pea, Bean or Lentil Soup, p. 52.]

NOTE—*This will also provide enough meat for Ham and Endive Mornay, p. 27.*

HOME-BAKED BEANS

2 *cups* (*1 pound*) *dried pea or navy beans*
1 *medium onion, peeled*
6 *slices lean bacon*
1 *cup strong coffee*
⅓ *cup molasses*
3 *or 4 tablespoons tomato paste*
1 *tablespoon mustard*   } *mixed together*
1 *tablespoon salt*
  freshly ground pepper

Soak the beans in water overnight.

Adding more water if necessary, cook the beans briskly, uncovered, for one hour, or until they are tender.

Preheat the oven to 275° F.

Put the onion and about a third of the beans into a 2-quart casserole and add 2 slices of bacon. Make two more layers, ending with bacon. Pour the coffee mixture over the beans and add water, if necessary, so that the liquid just covers the beans.

Cover and bake for at least six hours, checking occasionally, adding hot water if needed to keep the beans just barely covered and skimming off any fat that has risen to the surface. Remove the cover for the last hour of baking.

CINNAMON APPLESAUCE

Ideally, the applesauce for this January weekend should come straight from your freezer. If you don't have any on hand make applesauce, using 4 pounds of apples (McIntosh or tart green ones are best). Cut the apples into chunks and put them in a large pot. Add just enough water or apple juice to cover the bottom of the pot. Cover and cook gently, stirring frequently to keep the apples from sticking and burning. When the apples are soft, put them through a strainer or food mill. Discard the skins and cores. Sweeten the applesauce with brown sugar and add cinnamon to taste. Four pounds of apples will make about 6 cups of sauce.

APRICOT FOOL

Fruit fools—pureed fruits with thick cream—were probably served at Hampton Court in the time of Henry VIII. Recipes for them appear in the earliest English cookbooks, and their taste is as wonderful as their name.

1 pound dried apricots
½ cup brandy
sugar
1 cup heavy cream, whipped

Cover the dried apricots with water and cook them over moderate heat until they are very soft. Put the brandy and ½ cup of the apricot cooking liquid in the jar of an electric blender. Gradually blend the cooked apricots into the liquid. Add sugar to taste.

Serve small portions with a generous dab of unsweetened whipped cream.

This puree will keep indefinitely in the refrigerator.

SUNDAY LUNCH

Ham and Endive Mornay
Green Salad

·

Pot-Cheese Cake and Berries

HAM AND ENDIVE MORNAY

*6 large or 12 small Belgian endives (or 1 bunch of
    broccoli)*
butter
juice of 1 lemon (2–3 tablespoons)
salt and freshly ground pepper
approximately 1½ pounds cooked ham, thinly sliced

SAUCE MORNAY
    4 tablespoons butter
    4 tablespoons flour
1½ cups milk
    1 cup ham stock (from Braised Ham, p. 24)
    ¾ cup Swiss cheese, grated
        salt and freshly ground pepper
        pinch of nutmeg

27

If the endives are large, cut them in half lengthwise; if small, leave them whole. Melt some butter in a large, shallow casserole. Place the endives (or broccoli) in the casserole, in one layer if possible. Turn them in the butter over moderate heat until they are well coated, sprinkle them with salt, pepper and lemon juice, cover and cook over low heat until they are tender when pierced with a sharp knife (45 minutes to 1 hour, less for the broccoli).

Meanwhile, make the sauce. Melt the butter, add the flour and cook for a few minutes over low heat without browning, stirring constantly with a wire whisk. Add the milk and stock and stir rapidly over moderate heat until the sauce is thick and smooth. Add ½ cup of the cheese and stir until it is melted. Season the sauce to taste with salt, pepper and a pinch of nutmeg, and continue to cook it very slowly, stirring occasionally, for at least 15 minutes.

When the endives are tender, remove them from the casserole with tongs. Add the casserole juices to the sauce. Cover the bottom of the casserole with a thin layer of the sauce, add a layer of ham, place the endives on top of the ham and another layer of ham on the endives. Pour the remaining sauce over all, sprinkle with the rest of the cheese and place the casserole under a moderate broiler until the meat and vegetables are heated through and the sauce is lightly browned.

GREEN SALAD

A good green salad requires not the right recipe but the right approach. Don't decide what kinds of greens to buy until you are in the market and can see what is fresh and crisp. Try all the different greens that are available and mix them in any proportions. A tablespoon of coarsely chopped parsley or chives or a teaspoon or so of finely chopped herbs will make any salad taste better.

Wash the greens, shake off the water, cut or tear them into bite-sized pieces and lay them on a terry cloth towel. Roll the greens in the towel to dry them. If you refrigerate the greens in the towel, they will stay crisp for quite a few hours.

For six people, prepare six good handfuls of salad greens. Here is an excellent basic dressing:

BASIC DRESSING

juice of ½ lemon (about
1 ½ tablespoons)
4 *tablespoons olive oil* ⎤
1 *small clove garlic, minced* ⎱ *beaten together*
salt and freshly ground ⎰ *with a fork*
pepper ⎦

Menus for
FEBRUARY

FRIDAY DINNER

Bourride
Boiled Potatoes
Chicory Salad
·

Oranges in Kirsch

SATURDAY LUNCH

Celery and Olives
Grilled Cream Cheese
Sandwiches

·

Baked Apples

SATURDAY DINNER

Roast Leg of Lamb
Mustard Carrots
Turnip Puree

·

Chocolate Chip Cake

SUNDAY LUNCH

Aioli Lunch

·

Meringue Muffins Glacé

Preparation Schedule

for

FEBRUARY

There are good reasons to do some advance cooking for this weekend: not only will you have less work once the weekend begins but we've planned it so that you will be preparing two interrelated meals at the same time.

You will need some *aioli*, the focal point of Sunday's lunch, in order to prepare the sauce for Friday night's fish. Since the sauce requires 3 egg yolks, set them aside and use the whites to make *Meringue Muffins Glacé*, Sunday's dessert. You may fix the *aioli* and the muffins a day or two ahead—they both keep well, and you will have almost completed Sunday's meal before you even begin cooking on Friday night.

You can cook the *Mustard Carrots* for Saturday's dinner many days in advance. Bake the *Chocolate Chip Cake* any time from Friday morning on, or even earlier if you freeze it.

On Friday—After you buy the fish for the *Bourride* on Friday, you can prepare the *court bouillon*, or you can wait until dinner time, as long as it's ready an hour before you intend to serve. The *Oranges in Kirsch* should also be ready and chilling in the refrigerator an hour before dinner—you can prepare them even earlier if it's more convenient. Prepare the salad greens and the dressing. Start the potatoes boiling just before you begin to cook the fish.

On Saturday—Get the *Cream Cheese Sandwiches* ready for grilling while the apples are in the oven. Let the apples cool a bit while you grill the sandwiches.

The *Leg of Lamb* for Saturday's dinner should be seasoned and left to stand at room temperature for several hours before roasting. You can make the *Turnip Purée* any time Saturday afternoon, but wait until dinner time to add the egg whites.

On Sunday—On Sunday, if you have planned well, you will have some boiled potatoes and pieces of fish left from Friday's dinner to add to the vegetables you have selected for the *Aioli Lunch*.

FRIDAY DINNER

Bourride
Boiled Potatoes
Chicory Salad

·

Oranges in Kirsch

BOURRIDE

Bourride is a truly splendid dish—poached fish in a delicious, creamy sauce.

For the inexperienced cook, making *bourride* provides a perfect opportunity to learn three very useful cooking techniques: preparing a broth in which to poach fish (*court bouillon*), making mayonnaise, and poaching fish.

None of these techniques is complicated; you should be able to make the dish in a half hour if you prepare the *court bouillon* and the *aioli* (a garlic mayonnaise) in advance.

> 1 *recipe* court bouillon (see below)
> 3 *pounds cod, bass or any other large, firm-fleshed white fish, cut into steaks or thick fillets* (see note)
> 6 *medium potatoes or 12 new potatoes, boiled in their skins* (see note)
> 12 *slices French bread, toasted in the oven*

SAUCE

> 1 *cup* aioli (see below)
> 3 *egg yolks* (*use the egg whites for Meringue Muffins p. 45*)
> 1½ *cups* court bouillon (*after poaching fish*)

If you put the potatoes in to boil just before you begin cooking the fish, they will both be done at about the same time.

Bring the *court bouillon* to a boil in a Dutch oven, turn the heat down and when it is just simmering, put in the fish. Poach the fish *very* gently, keeping the broth barely simmering, until it is *just* done, 10–15 minutes depending on the thickness of the fish. Remove the pieces of fish very carefully with a slotted spoon, place them on a large platter (there will be lots of sauce) and keep them warm in a low oven. [Set aside the extra fish for the *Aioli Lunch,* p. 44.]

While the fish is cooking, beat the *aioli* and the egg yolks together in the top part of a double boiler. After the fish is cooked, put the *aioli* and yolks over just-boiling water and whisk in 1½ cups of the hot fish broth. Continue to beat almost constantly with the whisk until the sauce thickens, about 10 minutes. It will be very light and creamy. Remove the fish from the oven and pour the sauce over it.

To serve, put 2 slices of toast on a plate, cover it with a spoonful of sauce, then add the fish and several large spoonfuls of sauce. Serve with boiled potatoes.

NOTE—*Cook an extra pound of fish and 3 or 4 more medium potatoes if you intend to serve Aioli Lunch, p. 44, on Sunday. Make 3 cups of* aioli *by tripling the recipe below.*

COURT BOUILLON

fish trimmings and heads	
1 *stalk celery with leaves*	
1 *small onion, peeled*	
1 *bay leaf*	*simmered together, cov-*
1 *teaspoon salt*	*ered, for ½–1 hour and*
6 *peppercorns*	*then strained*
1 *cup dry white wine*	
1 *8-ounce bottle clam juice*	
3 *cups water*	

AIOLI (AND MAYONNAISE)

This gloriously garlicky sauce is good enough to build a meal around, as the French, who invented it, have known for ages. If you omit the garlic from *aioli* you will have a lovely homemade mayonnaise to be eaten plain or flavored with chopped or pureed herbs.

After alternating between the agony of the whisk and the somewhat imperfect sauce produced in a blender, we have concluded that only an electric beater will make a perfect *aioli* or mayonnaise with a minimum of elbow grease. You can also make a perfect *aioli* or mayonnaise with a whisk, of course, if you're feeling energetic. The rule to remember when you are making *aioli* or mayonnaise is that one egg yolk will absorb about 1 cup of oil. If you want to make 1½ cups of sauce, use 2 yolks—it's safer than trying to get more oil into 1 yolk. The recipe that follows will make 1 cup of *aioli*.

3 *large cloves garlic, minced*
1 *egg yolk, at room temperature*
  salt
  lemon juice or wine vinegar
1 *cup olive oil (the best quality you can get)*

Put the minced garlic in a mixing bowl and mash it against the sides to be sure it is completely reduced to a pulp. Add the egg yolk, a pinch of salt and 1 teaspoon of lemon juice or vinegar and beat at medium speed until the mixture is thick and sticky. Beating constantly at medium speed, add the first ½ cup of oil *a drop or two at a time,* making sure that each addition is completely absorbed by the yolk mixture before adding more oil. Add the rest of the oil in slightly larger quantities, continuing to beat constantly and moving the beater around in the bowl to make sure all the oil is absorbed. Reduce the speed of the beater as the *aioli* becomes very thick.

Taste the *aioli* (preferably on a piece of raw vegetable) and add another teaspoon or so of lemon juice or vinegar and a little more salt if necessary.

CHICORY SALAD

Malt vinegar has a good strong taste that seems to counteract the slight bitterness of some salad greens. Buy some if you see it, especially to use with chicory and escarole. If chicory is too bitter for your taste, mix it half and half with a milder green such as romaine lettuce.

Wash a head of chicory (about 1½ pounds), shake off as much water as possible, tear it into bite-sized pieces and lay it in one layer on a large terry towel. Roll it in the towel to dry it and put it in the refrigerator. Chicory can be kept for a day or two this way.

Just before serving, toss the chicory in this vinaigrette dressing:

> 1½ *tablespoons malt vinegar*
> *(or lemon juice)*
> 4 *tablespoons olive oil*
> 1 *small clove garlic, minced*
> ½ *teaspoon dried marjoram*
> *salt and freshly ground pepper*

beaten together well with a fork

ORANGES IN KIRSCH

This simple, elegant and delicious dessert is twice as good if Temple oranges are used—ask for them, if you don't see them.

6 *oranges*
1 *tablespoon sugar*
2 *ounces kirsch*

Peel the oranges with a very sharp knife and remove all of the white membrane. Cut them crosswise in thin slices, taking out the pits, and arrange them on a platter. Sprinkle them with sugar and half of the kirsch, cover and refrigerate them for at least 2 hours. Just before serving, sprinkle them with the remaining kirsch and be sure to spoon some juice over each portion as it is served.

SATURDAY LUNCH

Celery and Olives
Grilled Cream Cheese Sandwiches

·

Baked Apples

GRILLED CREAM CHEESE SANDWICHES

Toasted cheese sandwiches aren't all alike. Vary the fillings as much as you want, but cover them all with this light cream cheese custard for a fine, simple lunch.

1 *loaf French bread*
1 *pound cream cheese, at room temperature*
2 *or 3 eggs, lightly beaten*
1 *medium sweet onion, very finely chopped*

SUGGESTED FILLINGS
thin slices of smoked salmon or ham
sardines, tuna or salmon, mashed with a little lemon juice
  and mixed with small pieces of green pepper
anchovies and pimientos, cut in small pieces
mixed raw vegetables

Preheat the oven to 450° F.

Mash the cream cheese and combine it thoroughly with the eggs. Mix in the onion.

Mash the filling ingredients or cut them into small pieces.

Cut the bread in half lengthwise. Scoop out the soft center of the bread and put the filling in the cavity of each half. Cover the filling and the bread with a thick layer of the cream cheese mixture, put the sandwiches on a cookie sheet and bake them for about 15 minutes, until the topping is set and lightly browned.

Slice and serve immediately.

BAKED APPLES

6 apples (McIntosh or Rome Beauties)
brown sugar
butter

OPTIONAL ADDITIONS
brandy or sherry
raisins
nuts
horseradish

Preheat the oven to 350° F.

Core the apples, prick the skins a little to keep them from breaking while they bake and set them in a shallow baking dish or pie plate. Fill each apple with a teaspoon of brown sugar, a little butter and a splash of brandy or sherry, if you wish. Bake for 45 minutes to an hour. Serve with cream.

Baked apples are good stuffed with raisins or nuts or a combination of both, or with horseradish if they are to be served as an accompaniment to roast pork.

If you prefer apples baked without their skins, peel, core and quarter them and arrange the slices in a shallow baking dish. Sprinkle with brown sugar, dot with butter, add some brandy or sherry if you wish and bake, uncovered, for about 30 minutes.

SATURDAY DINNER

Roast Leg of Lamb
Mustard Carrots
Turnip Puree

·

Chocolate Chip Cake

ROAST LEG OF LAMB

Lamb should not be overcooked, of course, but it *will* be if you follow the directions on your meat thermometer. We prefer it pink and juicy (150° on the thermometer), but if you must have it well done, do not cook it beyond 165°. If you do not have fresh rosemary (or a few frozen sprigs from last summer's plant) be sure the dried herb is still fragrant—it rapidly loses its flavor.

1 *leg of lamb* (6–7 pounds)
4 *large cloves of garlic, cut into slivers*
  rosemary
  salt and freshly ground pepper

Preheat the oven to 350° F.

Pierce the meat an inch or so deep in 20 or more places and insert in each cut a sliver of garlic and a small sprig of fresh (or a pinch of dried) rosemary. Rub the meat all over with salt and pepper and roast it, allowing 12 minutes per pound (or until a meat thermometer registers 150°) for medium rare, 15 minutes per pound (or until a meat thermometer registers 165°) for well done.

MUSTARD CARROTS

The unusual taste of these carrots is impossible to describe. But we *can* tell you that carrots are always cheap and readily available, and that Mustard Carrots are easy to make and keep for weeks in the refrigerator. After you've tasted them you'll see why they'd be worth making even if they were expensive, hard to get, hard to make—and perishable.

MARINADE

½ cup white wine
½ cup wine vinegar
½ cup water
½ cup olive oil
1 clove garlic, minced
1 teaspoon salt   } mixed together in a saucepan
1 teaspoon sugar
1 bay leaf
3 sprigs fresh thyme or
      ½ teaspoon dried

1 pound carrots, scraped and cut in half crosswise and
      lengthwise
1½ teaspoons prepared mustard

Bring the marinade to a boil and add the carrots. Boil the carrots, uncovered, in the marinade until they are just tender when pierced with the sharp point of a knife. Cooking time will vary depending on the size and age of the carrots.

Remove the carrots to a shallow serving dish. Add the mustard to the marinade and blend it in well. Strain the marinade over the carrots and allow them to cool in it. Serve at room temperature.

TURNIP PUREE

2–3 *pounds small white turnips, peeled and sliced*
  3 *medium potatoes, peeled and sliced*
  1 *cup chicken broth*
  4 *tablespoons butter*
    salt and freshly ground pepper
  3 *egg whites (only if you have them left over)*

Put the turnips, potatoes and chicken broth in a large skillet or Dutch oven. Cover the pan, bring the liquid to a boil, lower the heat to moderate and cook the vegetables until they are tender and most of the liquid has been absorbed, about 20–25 minutes. Mash the vegetables with a potato masher if you like a slightly chunky mixture, or put them through a food mill for a fine puree.

Reheat just before serving, stirring in the butter and adding salt and pepper to taste.

If you have extra egg whites from the *Aioli*, p. 36, beat them until they are stiff but not dry and fold them into the cooled turnip puree a half hour before serving. Put the puree in a 2-quart casserole or soufflé dish and bake it at 350° for about 30 minutes, until the puree is puffed and lightly browned.

CHOCOLATE CHIP CAKE

The unsweetened chocolate chips in this light, brown-sugar cake come as a delicious surprise. Our thanks to Selma Laber for showing us how to make the cake her son has talked about for so many years.

½ *cup butter, softened*
  2 *cups brown sugar*
  3 *eggs, separated*
  2 *cups flour* ⎫
  1 *tablespoon baking soda* ⎭ *mixed together*
½ *cup sour cream* ⎫
½ *cup milk* ⎭ *mixed together*
  3 *squares unsweetened chocolate, cut into small pieces*
    (not grated)

Preheat the oven to 350° F.

Cream the butter and the brown sugar together and then blend in the egg yolks. Beat in the flour mixture alternately with the sour cream mixture and continue to beat until the batter is well blended. Beat the egg whites until they are stiff but not dry and fold them into the batter. Fold in the chocolate pieces. Pour the batter into 2 buttered 9-inch layer pans and bake for about 30 minutes, or until a toothpick inserted in the cake comes out clean.

Cool the layers and spread them with Chocolate Icing, using the recipe that follows. Plain or flavored whipped cream also makes an excellent icing for this cake.

CHOCOLATE ICING
> 3 *tablespoons butter*
> 8 *ounces semisweet chocolate*
> 1/4 *cup strong coffee or milk*
> 2 *teaspoons vanilla*
> 1–1 1/2 *cups confectioners' sugar*

Melt the butter and the chocolate in the top of a double boiler. Add the coffee or milk and beat well with an electric or hand beater. Beat in the vanilla and sugar to taste. Spread the icing while it is still warm.

SUNDAY LUNCH

Aioli Lunch

·

Meringue Muffins Glacé

AIOLI LUNCH

Make this dish as simple or as luxurious as you wish. It can be a light hors d'oeuvre, using three or four kinds of raw vegetables; a simple lunch, using boiled potatoes, tuna fish and raw carrots; or an elaborate feast including shrimp, lobster or crabmeat, artichoke hearts and raw mushrooms.

It is infinitely expandable—with a little extra *aioli*, you can turn this lunch into an informal buffet for a large group of people.

AIOLI
6 *large cloves garlic, minced*
2 *egg yolks, at room temperature*
  salt
  lemon juice or wine vinegar
2 *cups olive oil* (*the best quality you can get*)

Put the minced garlic in a mixing bowl and mash it against the sides to be sure it is completely reduced to a pulp. Add the egg yolks, a pinch of salt and 2 teaspoons of lemon juice or vinegar and beat at medium speed until the yolks are thick and sticky. Beating constantly at medium speed, add the first ½ cup of oil *a drop or two at a time*, making sure that each addition is completely absorbed by the yolks before adding more oil. Add the rest of the oil in slightly larger quantities, continuing to beat constantly and moving the beater around in the bowl to make sure all the oil is absorbed. Reduce the speed of the beater as the *aioli* becomes very thick. You will have about 2 cups of *aioli*.

Taste the *aioli* (preferably on a piece of raw vegetable) and add another teaspoon or two of lemon juice or vinegar and a little more salt if necessary.

Put the *aioli* in a bowl and place the bowl in the center of a large platter. Surround it with any combination of the following:

raw cauliflower, mushrooms, celery, carrots, turnip slices, fennel
artichoke hearts
boiled potatoes, hot or cold
hard-boiled eggs

tuna fish
crab meat, shrimp or lobster
cold meat, chicken or fish

MERINGUE MUFFINS GLACÉ

3 egg whites (see note)
¾ cup sugar
5 tablespoons cocoa

*coffee ice cream, or fresh blueberries or raspberries with
whipped cream*

Beat the egg whites until they are stiff. Very gradually beat in the
sugar and then gradually add the cocoa. Butter a muffin pan *very*
well and fill the cups ¾ full. Place in a cold oven, turn it to 250° F.
and bake for 1 hour.

Remove the pan from the oven and allow the muffins to cool for
about 10 minutes. Run a knife around the muffins before removing
them very carefully from the tin. The tops should be crisp and the
bottoms chewy.

Cut the top off each muffin just before serving. Fill it, either with
ice cream or with whipped cream and fruit. Replace the top.

This recipe will make 6 to 9 muffins, depending on the size of
your muffin tin.

NOTE—*Use the yolks in the* Bourride *sauce, p. 35.*

Menus for
MARCH

FRIDAY DINNER

Corned Beef and Cabbage
Carrots
Potatoes

·

Irish Coffee

SATURDAY LUNCH

Black Bean, Lentil or Pea Soup
Boston Lettuce Vinaigrette

·

Fresh Pineapple

SATURDAY DINNER

Chicken Breasts with Capers
Green Bean Puree
Watercress and Endive Salad

·

Chocolate Soufflé

SUNDAY LUNCH

Corned Beef Home Fries
Eggs

·

Coffee Cake

Preparation Schedule

for

MARCH

[ALL RECIPES SERVE 6]

Corned beef is as delicious as it is unpretentious. We use it here in three different and distinctive ways for a weekend which strikes a happy balance between the plain and the elegant.

In Advance—The only thing you ought to fix in advance for this weekend is the *Coffee Cake* for Sunday. It freezes well and can be reheated in a slow oven if you want to serve it warm.

On Friday—*Corned Beef and Cabbage* is a simple, one-pot meal. In the recipe, we give directions for cooking the meat in advance if necessary, but we prefer to cook it all on Friday. Remember to save the corned beef stock to make the soup on Saturday and be sure to soak the beans overnight on Friday.

On Saturday—*Black Bean Soup* needs about four hours to cook, *Lentil* and *Pea Soup* about two and a half. Whichever soup you're making, have it on the stove early on Saturday so that it will be ready in time for lunch.

You can make the *Green Bean Puree*, roll and skewer the chicken breasts and prepare the chocolate mixture for the soufflé early in the day on Saturday or in an hour of pre-dinner preparation. Once you have finished cooking the *Chicken Breasts with Capers*, arrange them on a platter, pour the butter sauce over them, put them in the oven and turn the heat on, setting it for 350° F. This way you can keep the chicken breasts warm while the oven is preheating—but don't leave them in for more than 10 minutes or they will be dry and overcooked. While the oven is heating, beat the egg whites and complete the batter for the *Chocolate Soufflé*. Put it in the oven and serve

49

the chicken and the vegetables. The soufflé will be ready just in time for dessert.

On Sunday—You should prepare the *Corned Beef Home Fries* on Sunday just before you plan to serve them. Allow a good 45 minutes to brown them properly and to fix the eggs.

FRIDAY DINNER

Corned Beef and Cabbage
Carrots
Potatoes

•

Irish Coffee

CORNED BEEF AND CABBAGE

4–5 *pounds corned beef* (see note)
  3 *large onions, peeled*
 12 *cloves garlic, peeled*
  6 *bay leaves*
 12 *peppercorns*
 ½ *pound carrots, scraped and cut in half*
  3 *pounds new potatoes in their skins or 3 pounds potatoes, peeled and cut into large chunks* (see note)
  1 *medium head cabbage, cut into wedges*

Place the corned beef, onions, garlic, bay leaves and peppercorns in a large pot and cover well with cold water. Bring the water to a boil, skim the top if necessary, turn down the heat and let the meat simmer slowly, covered, until it is tender, 3–4 hours. When the meat is done remove it from the pot, bring the stock to a racing boil and add the potatoes and carrots. After 20 minutes add the cabbage and continue to boil for 10 minutes, no more. The cabbage should still be very crisp. [Strain the broth and save it for Black Bean Soup, p. 52.]

While the vegetables are cooking, slice the meat and put it in the center of a large platter. When the vegetables are done, arrange them around the meat. Serve with plenty of butter for the vegetables and mustard and horseradish for the meat.

If you wish, you can cook the meat a day or two ahead, but be sure to save the stock so you can cook the vegetables in it.

NOTE—*You will need some extra meat and potatoes if you plan to make Corned Beef Home Fries, p. 58, on Sunday. The proportion of meat to potatoes depends on your preference, your pocketbook and what you have left. One extra pound of meat and 2 extra pounds of potatoes should do the job.*

IRISH COFFEE

Irish coffee is most attractive when served in wine glasses, but coffee mugs are certainly adequate. It's an adult dessert; serve crackers and Irish marmalade for the children.

> *sugar*
> *Irish whiskey (or Scotch)*
> 6 *cups strong black coffee*
> ½ *cup heavy cream, lightly whipped*

Put 1–2 teaspoons of sugar in each glass, add a shot of Irish whiskey and fill the glass with hot coffee, leaving at least ½ inch at the top. Stir well. Gently spoon whipped cream on top of the coffee so that it forms a half-inch layer. Serve immediately, without stirring.

SATURDAY LUNCH

Black Bean, Lentil or Pea Soup
Boston Lettuce Vinaigrette

·

Fresh Pineapple

BLACK BEAN SOUP

Corned beef stock is the basis of this soup and gives it its unique taste. You can also use the stock from Braised Ham, p. 24, which has a more subtle, but equally rich flavor. This basic recipe can also be used to make split pea or lentil soup, and we have included a few suggestions for these soups as well.

1 *pound dried black beans (or lentils or split peas)*
6 *cups corned beef stock plus 2 cups of water (or ham*
     stock, p. 24, with enough water added to make 2
     quarts)
1 *large onion, chopped*
3 *stalks celery, chopped*

SPECIAL INGREDIENTS
   for Black Bean Soup:
        about 1/2 cup sherry
        1 small onion, finely chopped
   for Lentil Soup:
        1 ten-ounce package frozen chopped spinach
        freshly grated Parmesan cheese
   for Pea Soup:
        sliced frankfurters
        croutons

Soak the beans overnight in cold water.

Put the stock, onion and celery in a large pot, add the drained beans, cover and simmer for about 4 hours, or until the beans are tender. Put about ⅓ of the beans through a food mill or a strainer and return them to the pot to thicken the soup. Season the soup to taste with sherry. (If you are using the ham stock, which already contains a good deal of wine, omit the sherry.) Since the broth is so flavorful and often quite salty, it seems unlikely that any additional seasoning will be necessary. Serve hot, garnished with chopped onion.

LENTIL SOUP

Lentils are delicious and, unlike dried beans or peas, they have the advantage of not needing to be soaked overnight. Add the frozen spinach—no need to defrost it—during the last half hour of cooking. This not only makes the soup look and taste better, but will reduce any excess saltiness in the broth which may not be absorbed by the lentils as easily as it is by the beans and the peas. Lentils need about 2 to 2½ hours to cook and the soup does not need thickening. Serve it with freshly grated Parmesan cheese.

PEA SOUP

You can use either yellow or green split peas. They will need overnight soaking, but will then cook in 2 to 2½ hours. Add some sliced frankfurters during the last half hour of cooking and serve with croutons, p. 143.

BOSTON LETTUCE VINAIGRETTE

1 large or 2 small heads Boston lettuce

DRESSING
1½ tablespoons wine vinegar
4 tablespoons olive oil
½ teaspoon salt
   freshly ground pepper   } *mixed together*
2 tablespoons fresh parsley,
   coarsely chopped

53

Boston lettuce makes a lovely, delicate salad—but it must be handled delicately, too. Gently peel the leaves from the head of lettuce, wash each one thoroughly under running water to remove any sand, shake off as much water as possible and lay the leaves in one layer on a large terry towel. Roll up the leaves in the towel and put them, towel and all, in the refrigerator until you are ready to toss the salad.

Just before serving, tear the leaves into bite-sized pieces and toss them in the dressing.

SATURDAY DINNER

Chicken Breasts with Capers
Green Bean Puree
Watercress and Endive Salad

·

Chocolate Soufflé

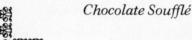

CHICKEN BREASTS WITH CAPERS

A sauce of butter, vinegar and capers is classic with brains and fish and makes a nice, piquant contrast with the delicate flavor of chicken breasts.

6 *whole chicken breasts, boned and skinned*
3 *ounces capers, bottled in vinegar*
1 *tablespoon flour* ⎫
  salt and freshly ground pepper ⎬ *mixed together*
  about 4 tablespoons butter for sautéeing ⎭

SAUCE

4 *tablespoons butter*
4 *tablespoons white vinegar*
   chopped parsley

Cut each chicken breast in half. Place the halves between two pieces of waxed paper and flatten them slightly by pounding them with the heel of your hand. Sprinkle them with a little salt and pepper and put 1 heaping teaspoon of capers near the wide end of each piece. Fold the chicken over the capers and roll it up like a jelly roll. Skewer the end with a toothpick. Coat each roll lightly with the flour mixture.

Heat the butter in a skillet and sauté the chicken rolls gently until they are very lightly browned on all sides. Cover the pan and cook them over low heat until the chicken is cooked through, about 15 minutes. Do not overcook. Remove the chicken to a platter, take out the toothpicks and keep it warm in a low oven.

Add the butter for the sauce to the juices in the pan. Melt it over low heat, scraping the bottom of the pan, and cook over medium heat until the butter is very hot. Do not let it burn. Remove the pan from the heat, stand back slightly (you'll see why), add the vinegar and stir the sauce well. Pour the sauce over the chicken, sprinkle with chopped parsley and serve immediately.

GREEN BEAN PUREE

2 *pounds green beans*
   butter
   salt and freshly ground pepper

Steam the beans according to the directions on p. 118. Do not over-cook. Let the beans cool until you can handle them.

Using the cooking liquid (and a little milk, if necessary) puree the beans quickly in an electric blender. The puree should be thick but not completely smooth—an occasional morsel of slightly crisp bean gives it a nice texture.

Before serving, heat the puree in the top of a double boiler with a lump of butter, salt and pepper.

WATERCRESS AND ENDIVE SALAD

1 *bunch watercress*
3 *large heads Belgian endive*

DRESSING
  4 *tablespoons olive oil*
1½ *tablespoons wine vinegar*
  ½ *clove garlic, minced* } *beaten together with a fork*
  ½ *teaspoon dried thyme*

Wash and trim the endives and cut them into 1½-inch pieces, separating the heads at the bottom. Cut the whole bunch of watercress in half crosswise. Toss the vegetables in the dressing just before serving.

CHOCOLATE SOUFFLÉ

Nothing is simpler or more elegant than a chocolate soufflé, and it has two great advantages—it can be made from ingredients one usually has on hand and it can be assembled in very little time.

If you are a novice when it comes to soufflés, just follow our directions and don't worry. It is only jealous chefs who have turned soufflé-making into such a formidable challenge. We have never had one fail us.

3 *tablespoons butter*
3 *tablespoons flour*
1 *cup milk*
¼ *teaspoon salt*
½ *cup sugar*
1½ *squares unsweetened chocolate, coarsely grated*
5 *egg yolks*
7 *egg whites*

½ *pint heavy cream, for whipping*

Melt the butter in the top of a double boiler over boiling water. Stir in the flour and cook for a minute or two. Gradually add the milk, stirring constantly until the mixture is smooth and thick. Stir in the salt and the sugar, then add the chocolate and continue to stir until the chocolate is completely melted and the sauce is thoroughly combined, creamy and thick.

Remove the sauce from the heat and let it cool slightly. Beat in the egg yolks. Let the sauce cool thoroughly. You may prepare it several hours in advance, if you wish.

The soufflé should be put in the oven just before you sit down to dinner. Preheat the oven to 350° F. Butter a 2-quart soufflé dish well and sprinkle it lightly with sugar. Beat the egg whites until they are stiff, but not dry. Fold a large spoonful of the egg whites into the chocolate sauce, then fold in the remaining egg whites lightly and rapidly.

Pour the batter into the soufflé dish and bake it for 30 minutes. Check to see if the soufflé is done. The perfect soufflé should be slightly moist inside, but it must not be runny. Test for doneness by shaking the dish a little while it is still in the oven; if the top shakes, the soufflé is still liquid underneath. If you have any doubt, leave it in the oven a little longer; a slightly dry soufflé is certainly better than a liquid one.

Do not take the soufflé out of the hot oven until you are ready to serve it. Whip the cream and get the serving dishes ready ahead of time, so that you can serve the soufflé as soon as it is done. Before you scoop into it, pierce the top in a few places with the serving spoon. This will allow some air to escape slowly, so that the soufflé will not drop precipitately when you start to serve it. Add a large spoonful or two of cold, unsweetened whipped cream to each serving.

SUNDAY LUNCH

Corned Beef Home Fries
Eggs

•

Coffee Cake

CORNED BEEF HOME FRIES

We'll choose this over corned beef hash any day.

>   *butter*
> *2 large onions, peeled and diced*
> *4–6 large or 10–12 small (new) cooked potatoes, peeled*
>   *and sliced*
>   *salt and freshly ground pepper*
>   *about 1 pound cooked corned beef (more, of course,*
>   *if you have it), cut into bite-sized pieces*

6–12 eggs

The secret here is to use lots of butter and to brown the potatoes very slowly.

Cook the onions in butter in a large skillet until they are transparent. Add the potatoes and brown them very slowly, using more butter when necessary. Season them carefully with salt and pepper—remember, you will be adding salty corned beef. When the potatoes are browned, about ½ hour, mix in the corned beef gently, continuing to cook until the meat is heated through.

Serve with poached or fried eggs.

COFFEE CAKE

1 cup sugar
½ cup butter, softened
2 eggs
2 cups flour
1 teaspoon baking powder
1 teaspoon baking soda   } *mixed together*
½ teaspoon ginger
1 cup sour cream
⅔ cup walnuts, coarsely chopped
⅔ cup raisins

TOPPING
1 tablespoon butter
¼ cup sugar
1½ tablespoons flour   } *worked together with your fingers to a crumb-like texture*
½ teaspoon cinnamon
½ cup walnuts, coarsely chopped

Preheat the oven to 350° F.

Cream the sugar and butter together. Beat in the eggs, one at a time. Stir in the dry ingredients and the sour cream alternately. Add the nuts and raisins.

Put the batter in a buttered 9- by 9-inch pan. Cover with the topping and bake it for about 45 minutes, until a toothpick inserted at the center comes out clean.

Serve warm or cool.

Menus for
APRIL

FRIDAY DINNER

Borshch
Pirozhki
Green Salad

·

Paskha

SATURDAY LUNCH

Zakuski:
  Eggs a la Russe
  Pickled Herring
  Pickled Mushrooms
  Eggplant Caviar
  Cucumber Salad
  Cold Pirozhki

·

Black Bread and Honey
Tea

SATURDAY DINNER

Brisket of Beef in Dill Sauce
Kasha
Steamed Cauliflower

·

Kisel

SUNDAY LUNCH

Blini with Red Caviar
and Sour Cream

·

Paskha

Preparation Schedule

for

APRIL

[ALL RECIPES SERVE 6]

All of our weekends are special, but this weekend is *very* special. The food is Russian—hearty, varied, exotic but not fancy— familiar enough to tempt the most reluctant American palate. This is a very good way for people to find out how much they like Russian food, if they have not had a chance to know before.

If you want to turn this weekend-long feast into a celebration, serve some chilled vodka and good black caviar before dinner.

This weekend's menus call for a lot of advance cooking, so choose a week when you're in the right mood and start three or four days ahead so you won't be rushed. While you're busy cooking remember that you can look forward to a weekend of good food and little work.

In Advance—The first thing to make is the *Borshch* for Friday night's dinner. It requires a minimum of five hours of cooking time, but don't be put off by this: it does not have to be tended during much of this time, the cooking process can be interrupted and resumed at several stages and, in cooking the *Borshch*, you will also be preparing the *Brisket of Beef* for Saturday's dinner. Make the *Borshch* three or four days in advance, if possible, to allow its full flavor to develop, taking it out of the refrigerator and reheating it once during this period, if you have a chance. Slice the brisket when it is cool and refrigerate or freeze it.

Making the *Pirozhki* is the other major task for the week; you can make them on Thursday and refrigerate them, or fix them well in advance and freeze them. The *Paskha* should also be made on Thursday; this simply involves combining ingredients and putting them into a mold.

You can make the *Eggplant Caviar* and the *Pickled Mush-*

rooms in advance, too, and they will keep for days. The *Kisel* can be fixed at any time, as long as you allow at least three hours for it to gel.

On Friday—All you will have to do on Friday is make a salad.

On Saturday—On Saturday morning fix the *Eggs a la Russe* and the *Cucumber Salad* for lunch. The *Kasha*, *Dill Sauce* and *Cauliflower* for Saturday's dinner can be prepared in about 30 minutes while the brisket is being heated.

On Sunday—Start preparing the *Blini* on Sunday about an hour before you plan to serve them. They'll take 20–30 minutes to rise, and you'll need time to cook all the *Blini* once the batter is ready.

This weekend's menus may sound a bit like production plans for a Soviet Stakhanovite worker, rather than suggestions for a casual American cook. If you want to simplify them a bit, you can serve fruit instead of *Paskha*, pumpernickel instead of *Pirozhki*, red caviar omelettes instead of *Blini*, but we hope you won't. We have prepared these menus many times ourselves and have always felt it was well worth the effort.

FRIDAY DINNER

Borshch
Pirozhki
Green Salad

·

Paskha

BORSHCH

Borshch is probably what most Americans think of first when Russian food is mentioned, yet there are almost as many different versions of borshch as there are Russian cooks. We find the cold beet soup which is so popular here one of the less interesting of them. The one we present is hot and blends robust peasant ingredients—cabbage, tomatoes and meat as well as beets—in a wondrously complex and subtle brew. Borshch should be made at least a day in advance, three or four if possible, to allow its flavor to develop fully.

We serve it as a main course—no explanations necessary.

 3 *pounds marrow bones*
3½ *pounds flanken, or other soup meat*
 1 *large onion, peeled*
 6 *large sprigs fresh dill*
 2 *bay leaves*
   salt and freshly ground pepper
 2 *carrots, cut in chunks*
 1 *large can Italian plum tomatoes (about 4 cups)*
[5 *pounds brisket of beef, after trimming* (see note)]
   Juice of 3 or more lemons
   about 2½ tablespoons sugar
 1 *head white cabbage, about 2½ pounds, coarsely shredded*
 1 *one-pound can beets, cut in small pieces*

   sour cream
   chopped dill

Make a stock by placing the bones, soup meat, onion, dill, bay leaves, 1 tablespoon of salt and some freshly ground pepper in a large soup pot. Cover these ingredients with 3 quarts of water, bring it all to a boil and simmer, covered, for about an hour, skimming off any scum that rises to the surface.

Add the carrots and tomatoes [and brisket] to the stock, season with the juice of 3 lemons and 2½ tablespoons of sugar, and simmer, covered, for 2 or 3 hours [or until the brisket is just tender]. Remove the bones and soup meat [and brisket] from the pot and add the cabbage, beets and beet juice. Cut the soup meat into bite-sized pieces and put it back in the pot. [Wrap the brisket in foil and refrigerate it.] Bring the soup to a boil, cover, lower the heat and simmer for another hour or so.

Refrigerate, overnight at least.

Several hours before serving, remove any fat that has congealed on the surface and reheat the *Borshch* over low heat. Taste for seasoning. The *Borshch* will most likely need a good deal more salt before you can properly judge its sweet and sour flavor. Add a little more sugar if the *Borshch* is too sour, more lemon juice, or a splash of vinegar, if it is too sweet. Continue simmering and tasting until ready to serve.

Put a dollop of sour cream and a sprinkling of chopped fresh dill in each bowl of soup.

NOTE—*Cook the brisket in the* Borshch *if you are planning to serve* Brisket of Beef in Dill Sauce, *p. 73. This will not only save time, but will add good flavor to both the* Borshch *and the brisket.*

PIROZHKI

These delicious little pastries, a classic Russian accompaniment to a variety of soups, may be served hot or at room temperature. They can be made with a number of different fillings and are equally appropriate as an appetizer, on the lunch table, or as part of a cocktail party buffet.

As with all small pastries, *pirozhki* take some time and patience to prepare, but they can be made in advance and frozen, baked or unbaked, or they may be refrigerated for a day or two and then reheated. If you are pressed for time, try making fewer large ones, instead of many small ones. Some people might prefer a single *pirozhok* (pee-rawzh-AWK, *s.*) to several *pirozhki* (pee-rawzh-KEE, *pl.*).

PASTRY

    2 *cups flour*
       pinch of salt
   ¾ *cup cold butter, cut into small pieces*
  4–6 *tablespoons sour cream*

FILLING (see note)

      butter
    1 *large onion, finely chopped, or about 1 cup finely chopped shallots*
   ¾ *pound mushrooms, washed and chopped*
      salt and freshly ground pepper
      dry mustard
      sherry

    1 *egg, beaten with 2 tablespoons milk*

To make the pastry, put the flour and the salt in a bowl, add the butter and work it into the flour with a pastry blender or your fingers until it has the consistency of coarse meal. Stir in the sour cream with a fork, adding just enough so that the mixture holds together. Form the dough into a ball, wrap it in waxed paper or foil and refrigerate it while you prepare the filling.

Melt some butter in a large skillet, add the onions or shallots and sauté them until they are golden brown. Add the mushrooms to the onions, season them with salt, pepper and a pinch or two of dry mustard and continue to cook until the liquid from the mushrooms has evaporated. Add 1 or 2 tablespoons of sherry and cook over low heat for another five minutes or so, until the liquid is absorbed.

Preheat the oven to 400° F.

Roll out the dough on a well-floured board and cut it into rounds with the rim of a glass about 3″ in diameter. Place about a teaspoon of filling near the center of each pastry circle. Fold the pastry in half and press the edges together with a fork. Place the pastries side by side on a cookie sheet, brush them with the beaten egg and milk mixture and bake them until they are golden brown, about 15 minutes. If you bake them in advance, reheat them in a moderate oven.

This recipe will make about 48 small *pirozhki*. It may sound like a lot for six people, but you'll be surprised to see how quickly they disappear, especially if you put the leftovers on the *zakuski* table on Saturday.

NOTE—*If you are planning to make* Kasha *with mushrooms and onions, p. 74, you may find it convenient to make a double amount of this filling and to set aside about half of it to use in the* Kasha.

GREEN SALAD

Choose the freshest, crispest salad greens you can find. Wash them under running water and dry them by rolling them in a large terry towel. Break the greens into bite-sized pieces and toss them with Vinaigrette Dressing just before serving.

VINAIGRETTE DRESSING
- 1½ tablespoons wine vinegar
- 4 tablespoons olive oil
  salt and freshly ground pepper
- 1 shallot or scallion, finely chopped or 1 small clove garlic, minced

Combine all the ingredients and beat well with a fork.

PASKHA

Paskha is the traditional Russian Easter dessert. The arduousness of the Russian Orthodox Lent, requiring abstinence not only from meat but from all animal products, accounts for the luxurious richness of this dessert that crowns the Easter feast. *Paskha* merges cream, cheese, butter, eggs, nuts and fruit into one glorious whole.

A new clay flowerpot makes a charming mold for *paskha* and is often used in the absence of a traditional *paskha* mold.

Paskha keeps well in the refrigerator and can be made several days in advance. (*See note.*)

¾ cup sour cream
¼ cup heavy cream
1 teaspoon vanilla
2 hard-boiled egg yolks
1½ pounds (3 cups) farmer cheese
¾ cup butter, at room temperature
1½ cups confectioners' sugar
⅓ cup almonds, blanched and chopped
⅓ cup dried currants

Beat the sour cream, cream and vanilla together in a large bowl. Add the hard-boiled egg yolks, farmer cheese, butter and sugar, beating until they are well combined. Fold in the almonds and currants.

Line a 7-inch clay flowerpot or a 1½-quart mold with damp cheesecloth, allowing the cheesecloth to hang over the edges. Pack the mixture into the mold and fold the cheesecloth over the top. Press a plate on top of the *paskha* and weight it down with a stone or heavy can. Refrigerate overnight.

The *paskha* may be unmolded several hours before serving. Invert the pot on a plate and use the cheesecloth to facilitate unmolding. Remove the cheesecloth and decorate the *paskha* with toasted almonds, currants, candied fruits or strawberries. Serve small portions—it is very rich.

NOTE—*We intend the* paskha *to be served twice during our Russian weekend; this recipe will easily serve 12. The* paskha *can be remolded after it has been served the first time, using a smaller mold and lining it as before with damp cheesecloth.*

SATURDAY LUNCH

Zakuski:
> *Eggs a la Russe*
> *Pickled Herring*
> *Pickled Mushrooms*
> *Eggplant Caviar*
> *Cucumber Salad*
> *Cold Pirozhki*

.

Black Bread and Honey
Tea

ZAKUSKI

Zakuski—Russian appetizers—are usually served with vodka before a large meal. We serve them as a lunch.

You may add whatever you wish to the *zakuski* table: olives, cherry tomatoes, pickles or relishes, or any appropriate cooked foods you may have in your refrigerator. You can buy Pickled Herring at most delicatessen counters or in jars at a supermarket. Get some in wine sauce and some in cream sauce; it's delicious both ways.

Make all or just some of the dishes for which we give recipes. If you decide to make them all, reduce the quantities of each slightly. Variety is the point, but remember—just a little of each.

EGGS A LA RUSSE

SAUCE

1 cup sour cream
1 teaspoon prepared mustard
   dash of chili sauce   } mixed together
2 tablespoons fresh dill,
   finely cut
2 tablespoons milk or cream,
   approximately
1 tablespoon fresh dill,
   finely cut

6 eggs, hard-boiled and sliced in half lengthwise
1 can flat anchovy filets

Thin the sauce slightly with milk or cream until it has the consistency of thick buttermilk. Spoon a thin layer of sauce onto a serving platter. Arrange the eggs on the sauce, yolks down, and place a
strip of anchovy on each egg. Spoon the remaining sauce over the
eggs so that they are thinly but completely covered. Before serving,
sprinkle with the remaining dill.

PICKLED MUSHROOMS

MARINADE

½ cup dry white wine
¼ cup wine vinegar
¼ cup olive oil
1 large clove garlic, sliced
1 large bay leaf
2–3 sprigs fresh rosemary or thyme (or ¼ teaspoon dried)
   salt and freshly ground pepper

1 pound fresh mushrooms, whole or sliced

Bring the marinade ingredients to a boil in a large skillet and
simmer for 10–15 minutes. Stir in the mushrooms, cover the pan

and simmer for 10 minutes more, stirring occasionally. Put the mushrooms in a jar or covered bowl just large enough to hold them. Strain the juices over them and let them marinate for at least 24 hours.

Serve the mushrooms at room temperature. They will keep for several weeks in the refrigerator.

EGGPLANT CAVIAR

> 1 large eggplant
> 1 green pepper, seeded and chopped
> 1 small onion, peeled and chopped
> 1 tomato, peeled and chopped
> 2–3 tablespoons olive oil
> Juice of ½ lemon (about 1½ tablespoons)
> salt and freshly ground pepper

Preheat the oven to 350° F.

Put the eggplant in a pan and bake it until it is tender—about 1 hour. Chop or grind together the unpeeled eggplant, pepper, onion and tomato. Add the oil and lemon juice and season to taste with salt and pepper. Mix well. Serve at room temperature.

Eggplant caviar will keep for about two weeks in the refrigerator.

CUCUMBER SALAD

DRESSING

> ⅓ cup vinegar
> ⅔ cup water
> 2 teaspoons sugar
> 1 tablespoon chopped fresh dill   } mixed together
> salt and freshly ground pepper

> 6 cucumbers, peeled and thinly sliced
> 1 sweet onion, peeled and thinly sliced

Pour the dressing over the cucumbers and onion and refrigerate them for at least 2 hours.

SATURDAY DINNER

Brisket of Beef in Dill Sauce
Kasha
Steamed Cauliflower

·

Kisel

BRISKET OF BEEF IN DILL SAUCE

Cut the brisket which was cooked in the *Borshch* into thin slices, arrange them on a platter, cover it with foil and heat in a 250° F. oven while preparing the sauce. (Any pot-roasted meat may be used with this sauce.)

DILL SAUCE
> 3 *tablespoons butter*
> 1 *large clove garlic, minced*
> 3 *tablespoons flour*
> 3 *cups beef broth*
> 1 *teaspoon lemon juice*
> 1½ *teaspoons vinegar*
> 1½ *teaspoons sugar*
> 3 *tablespoons fresh dill, finely chopped*
> *salt and freshly ground pepper*

Melt the butter in a saucepan or medium-sized skillet, add the garlic and cook it over low heat for a few seconds without letting it

73

brown. Stir in the flour and cook, stirring, for a minute or two, then gradually add the broth, stirring constantly with a wire whisk until thoroughly blended. Cook the sauce over moderate heat, stirring from time to time, until it thickens slightly. Season it with the lemon juice, vinegar, sugar, dill, salt and pepper. Pour some of the sauce over the meat and serve the rest in a pitcher or bowl.

This sauce may be prepared in advance. When you reheat it, thin it with additional broth if necessary and readjust the seasonings.

KASHA

Kasha, roasted brown buckwheat groats, is a staple of the Russian peasant diet. It has a distinctive, nutlike flavor.

1 *large onion, peeled*
 and diced
 butter
¾ *pound mushrooms,*
 sliced

(or extra mushroom filling
from Pirozhki, *p. 67*

1 *egg, lightly beaten*
1 *cup coarse* kasha
2 *cups beef broth, heated to the boiling point*
 salt and freshly ground pepper

Sauté the onion in butter in a pot or a large skillet until it begins to brown, add the mushrooms and continue to cook for two or three minutes. [If you have extra *Pirozhki* filling, p. 67, omit the onions and mushrooms and sauté the extra filling in butter.] Stir the egg into the *kasha* and combine it with the onions and mushrooms in the pot. Cook, adding more butter if necessary and stirring constantly, until the *kasha* grains separate and are lightly toasted. Add the broth, cover and cook over low heat until all the liquid has been absorbed, about 30 minutes. Season with butter, salt and pepper before serving.

STEAMED CAULIFLOWER

Wash a large bunch of cauliflower and cut it into serving pieces.

Bring about 2 inches of salted water to a rapid boil in a large pot, put in the cauliflower, stem ends down, cover the pot and cook the cauliflower rapidly until the thick stems are tender when pierced with the point of a sharp knife, about 10 or 15 minutes. Drain it well before serving.

Remember when you are cooking the cauliflower that it is always better to undercook than to overcook it. At worst, it will be just a bit crunchier than you planned—lots of people prefer it that way.

Leftover cauliflower can be used to make a lovely cold salad. Cut it up, sprinkle it with a good pinch of oregano and toss it in a garlicky vinaigrette dressing.

KISEL

Kisel is a tart fruit dessert usually made with potato starch, which gives it a somewhat gluey consistency. This is our own adaptation, an improvement, we believe, on the traditional *kisel*.

2 cups cranberry juice
1 package unflavored gelatin, dissolved in ¼ cup water
1 10-ounce box frozen raspberries

½ cup heavy cream, for whipping

Heat one cup of the cranberry juice to the boiling point. Add the gelatin and stir until it is completely dissolved. Remove the pot from the heat and add one cup of cold cranberry juice. Pour the gelatin mixture into a serving bowl and add the frozen raspberries, breaking them apart with a fork. Refrigerate the *kisel* until it has set, about 3 hours.

Stir the *kisel* a little before serving, topped with unsweetened whipped cream.

SUNDAY LUNCH

Blini with Red Caviar and Sour Cream

·

Paskha

BLINI WITH RED CAVIAR AND SOUR CREAM

Yeast makes these buckwheat pancakes very special and very unlike the familiar American ones. Some purists insist that making *blini* is a 6-hour production, which would preclude them from anybody's weekend, but we've gotten the rising time down to a mere 20 minutes and the *blini* are superb.

  1 *package dry yeast or 1 cake compressed yeast*
2¼ *cups warm milk*
  1 *tablespoon melted butter*
  2 *eggs, separated*
  1 *cup white flour*   } *or 1½ cups white flour*
 ½ *cup buckwheat flour*
 ¾ *teaspoon salt*
  1 *teaspoon sugar*

    melted butter
    sour cream
    red caviar

76

Dissolve the yeast thoroughly in a little of the warm (not hot) milk in a large mixing bowl. Add the rest of the milk, the butter and egg yolks. Mix the dry ingredients together, add them to the liquid mixture, and whisk the batter until it is perfectly smooth. Beat the egg whites until they are stiff but not dry and fold them into the batter. Cover the bowl with a dish towel and put it in a warm place for 20–30 minutes.

Cook the pancakes on a buttered griddle and keep them warm on a platter in a very low oven until all the batter has been used.

Serve the *blini* with a small pitcher of melted butter and some sour cream and red caviar.

Menus for
MAY

FRIDAY DINNER

*Chopped Liver with
Grated Black Radish
Chicken Soup with
Chicken and Matzoh Balls
Challah*

·

Mandelbroit

SATURDAY LUNCH

Pickled Shrimp and Onions
Tomato Aspic

·

Cantaloupe

SATURDAY DINNER

Spicy Pork
Persian Rice
Watercress and Tomato Salad

·

Mocha Nut Cake

SUNDAY LUNCH

Asparagus Hollandaise
Chicken Salad

·

Strawberries and Double Cream

Preparation Schedule

for

MAY

[ALL RECIPES SERVE 6]

Cool nights and warm days—warm dinners and cool lunches. Here are four splendid meals for the lovely month of May.

Each recipe for the Friday night Jewish dinner is truly authentic, but our approach is slightly unorthodox. The traditional meal is a fine example of how to get the most from a chicken: the chicken, which is also the main course, produces the liver and the soup as well as the chicken fat which is essential to the flavor of the matzoh balls, the chopped liver and the grated radish. Adapting this ancient formula to modern tastes and packaging customs, we serve generous helpings of chopped liver, use the soup as the main course and save most of the chicken for Sunday's lunch. One tradition we don't tamper with —we always serve the beautiful, braided egg bread, *challah*.

In Advance—With the exception of the *Matzoh Balls*, which can be made in advance but will be lighter and fluffier if cooked some time on Friday, everything for Friday's dinner should be prepared several days in advance. You can make the *Chicken Soup* and the *Chicken* and render the *Chicken Fat* well in advance. If you can, make some extra soup and put it in the freezer and render some extra fat and keep it in the refrigerator. Once you get used to having these available, it's hard to do without them. Make the *Chopped Liver*, the *Grated Black Radish* and the *Mandelbroit* a few days ahead.

On Friday—The meals for the rest of the weekend are surprisingly simple, but they require some thought and a little work in advance. The *Matzoh Balls*, of course, should be made on Friday. Make the *Double Cream* for Sunday on Friday, too, as it needs time in the refrigerator to thicken; you can even make it a week or two ahead if you want. Put the *Shrimp and Onions* in the sauce on Friday—they should marinate for 24 hours. You can make the *Tomato Aspic* on Friday or on Saturday morning, as long as you allow 3 hours for it to gel. Season the *Spicy Pork* roast for Saturday night on Friday.

On Saturday—Mocha Nut Cake takes less time to prepare than any layer cake we know and can easily be left for Saturday, but, if you wish, you can bake it far in advance and freeze it.

Put the rice in to soak on Saturday morning. Two and a half hours before you intend to serve dinner, prepare the *Persian Rice* and begin steaming it. Put the tomatoes for the *Tomato and Watercress Salad* in the marinade, the roast in the oven and the topping on the cake. Have a relaxed cocktail hour or two—your dinner will tend itself.

On Sunday—Prepare Sunday's lunch on Sunday morning. Fix the *Chicken Salad* whenever it's convenient and wash the *Strawberries*. Make the *Hollandaise Sauce* up to an hour before serving time and let it sit over warm water while you cook the *Asparagus*.

There's no denying it—there's an awful lot of cooking to be done for this weekend. All the dishes are so good that it's hard to decide what to leave out if you feel you just can't fix everything in the menus, but our suggestion is to cook the dinners and change the lunches as follows:

Fix some extra chopped liver and serve it in rye bread sandwiches for lunch on Saturday. On Sunday, omit the Hollandaise Sauce and serve the asparagus at room temperature with a vinaigrette dressing. Use the chicken in sandwiches instead of in a salad. The strawberries will be delicious for dessert—even with plain old cream.

FRIDAY DINNER

Chopped Liver with Grated Black Radish
Chicken Soup with Chicken
and Matzoh Balls
Challah

·

Mandelbroit

CHOPPED LIVER

Chopped liver is most frequently served on crackers as an hors d'oeuvre. It is often hard to maintain the delicate balance between eating as much of it as you want and eating too much to enjoy the meal that follows. We have tried to avoid such problems in this Friday night meal. The chopped liver is intended as a substantial first course—serve generous portions.

This recipe assumes that you are using previously rendered chicken fat. However, you can easily prepare chopped liver while you are rendering chicken fat (see below), if you happen to be doing both on the same day. The onions can be browned in the fat and added, with the *gribenes*, to the chopped liver.

> *about 6 tablespoons rendered chicken fat* (see below)
> 3–4 *medium onions, peeled and diced*
> 1 *pound chicken livers (about 15 livers)*
> 4–6 *hard-boiled eggs*
> *salt and freshly ground pepper*

Heat half the chicken fat in a large frying pan, add the onions, sprinkle them with salt and pepper and cook them until they are very well browned. Remove the onions from the pan, add the livers, season them with salt and pepper and cook them over moderate heat until they are cooked through. Chop the onions, the *gribenes* (if you have any), the chicken livers and the eggs, or put them through a meat grinder. Combine them in a bowl, adding the pan juices. Mash them all together, adding lots of salt and pepper and enough additional chicken fat so that the chopped liver is moist but not mushy.

Serve the chopped liver as an appetizer on a bed of greens, garnished with Grated Black Radish, p. 85, or with raw carrots and radishes.

TO RENDER CHICKEN FAT

Chicken fat is an essential ingredient in three of the recipes for this Friday dinner—Chopped Liver, p. 83, Grated Black Radish, p. 85, and Matzoh Balls, p. 86. You can sometimes buy rendered chicken fat, either from a butcher or in a jar in the Jewish foods section of a supermarket. It is, however, so easy to render chicken fat and it fills the house with such a delicious smell that it is well worth taking a very little extra trouble to prepare it yourself.

Collect and freeze pieces of raw fat each time you prepare chicken until you have enough to render, or ask the butcher for some. One pound of raw chicken fat will produce about two cups of rendered fat.

Cut the raw fat into very small pieces and cook it over very low heat in a large skillet until the fat has melted and the small pieces (*gribenes*) are crisp and brown. Remove the *gribenes*, add a diced onion to the pan (several if you are also preparing Chopped Liver, p. 83), and cook the onion until it is well browned. Let the rendered fat cool a bit, strain it into a jar, cover and refrigerate it. It will keep indefinitely in the refrigerator. Drain the browned onions and *gribenes*. They are delicious in chopped liver, or they can be sprinkled with salt and served as a snack with drinks.

Chicken fat is very useful in cooking and adds a unique flavor to many different kinds of dishes. Use it in mashed potatoes, or instead of butter when browning onions or meat. Best of all, spread it on a piece of fresh rye bread or pumpernickel, add a slice of raw onion and have a good *nosh!*

GRATED BLACK RADISH

Black radishes are about the size and shape of turnips and once you've peeled off their rich black skins they're about the same color, too. Their texture is very unlike that of the familiar red radish and they are mild rather than pungent. Peeled, grated and seasoned with chicken fat they make an unusual relish to serve with chopped liver.

Mix ½ pound of grated radishes with about ½ cup of chicken fat. Season with salt and that's all there is to it. Grated black radish will keep for weeks in the refrigerator.

CHICKEN SOUP

People like this chicken soup so much they often wish they could make a meal of it, and so we are suggesting just that.

It is no extra trouble to make this soup in large quantities; we strongly recommend this since it freezes exceptionally well and it is wonderful to have a supply of first-rate chicken soup or stock on hand. If you omit the chicken meat and add a few more backs and necks, you will still have an excellent stock for use as a base for soups and sauces.

3–4 *pounds chicken necks, backs and giblets*
  1 *onion, peeled*
  2 *carrots*
  2 *stalks celery with leaves*
    a few sprigs fresh dill
    a few sprigs fresh parsley
  2 *or 3 peppercorns*
    salt
  4 *quarts water*
    about 3 pounds chicken parts or 1 small chicken
      (*about 3½ pounds*) (*see note*)

Put the chicken backs, necks and giblets and all the vegetables in a very large pot. Add the water, the peppercorns and some salt. Bring it all to a boil, skim the surface if necessary, and let it simmer, covered, for about an hour. Add the chicken parts or chicken and continue to simmer until the chicken is cooked through. This will take about 20 minutes for chicken parts, 30–40 minutes for a whole, small chicken. Remove the chicken from the pot and let it cool while the backs, necks, giblets and vegetables continue to simmer. When the chicken is cool, remove the meat from the bones and return the bones and skin to the pot. Continue to simmer, partially covered, for about another hour or more, the longer the better.

Cut the chicken into bite-sized pieces and refrigerate it. [Set aside 5 cups of chicken for Chicken Salad, pp. 95–96. You will have about 3 cups of chicken left for the soup.]

Strain the broth, cut up the carrots and put them and the remaining cut-up chicken (about 3 cups) into the soup before refrigerating.

Before serving, remove the fat from the surface of the soup. (This will be easy to do if the soup has been refrigerated and the fat has solidified.) Heat the Matzoh Balls in the soup and sprinkle each portion with chopped dill or parsley.

This recipe will make 3½–4 quarts of soup, more than enough to serve 6 people as a main course.

NOTE—*Use 5 more lbs. of chicken if you plan to make Chicken Salad, pp. 95–96, and reserve 5 cups of cooked, diced chicken for this purpose.*

MATZOH BALLS

Known in Yiddish as *knaidlach,* these dumplings are traditionally served with chicken soup. They are hard to describe, since they're quite unlike any other kind of dumpling—but if you've never tried them before, you are in for a treat.

    3 *eggs*
1¼ *cups water*
1½ *teaspoons salt*
    1 *heaping tablespoon solidified chicken fat*
    2 *cups matzoh meal*

Beat the eggs thoroughly, beat in the other ingredients in the order given, and refrigerate it all, covered, for at least one hour.

Bring about 5 inches of salted water to a boil in each of 2 large pots. Form the matzoh-meal mixture into walnut-sized balls and lower them with a slotted spoon into the gently boiling water, using both pots so that the dumplings are not overcrowded. Each *knaidle* should have room to rise to the water's surface and cook there.

Let the matzoh balls cook in the gently boiling water for about 30 minutes. Then remove one from the water and cut it through the center to see if it is done—it should be light and fluffy throughout. If the matzoh balls are not quite done, continue to cook them for another few minutes, but watch them carefully because they will fall apart if they are overcooked.

When the matzoh balls are done, remove them from the water with a slotted spoon and drain them on paper towels. Reheat them in the soup before serving.

You will have about 30 matzoh balls.

MANDELBROIT

Mandelbroit—literally "almond bread"—is a slightly sweet, crunchy toast, full of nuts. It will keep for weeks in an airtight container and is a very pleasant accompaniment to tea or sherry.

> 2 *eggs*
> ½ *cup vegetable oil*
> 6 *tablespoons sugar*
> 1½ *cups flour*
> *pinch of salt*
> *grated rind of ½ lemon*
> ¾ *cup slivered almonds, preferably toasted* (see note)

Preheat the oven to 350° F.

Beat the eggs with a fork and then blend in the rest of the ingredients in the order given. The texture of the dough will be unfamiliar —it may seem too soft to form into a loaf, but it's not.

Put the dough on an ungreased cookie sheet, form it into a long, narrow loaf and make diagonal slits every ½ inch along the top of the loaf with a knife. Bake the *mandelbroit* for 45 minutes, then remove it from the oven and cut it, through the slits on the top, into ½-inch slices. Return the slices to the oven to toast until they are golden brown, about 10 minutes on each side.

NOTE—*Toast a full cup of slivered almonds, if you plan to make Jeri Laber's Chicken Salad, p. 96.*

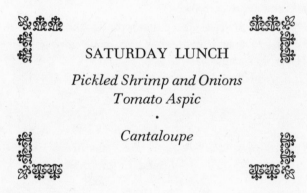

SATURDAY LUNCH

Pickled Shrimp and Onions
Tomato Aspic

•

Cantaloupe

PICKLED SHRIMP AND ONIONS

You will wonder what alchemy turns these simple ingredients into such a special dish.

> *garlic cloves*
> *mixed pickling spices*
> 2 *pounds shelled shrimp (2½ pounds unshelled)*
> 1 *large Bermuda onion, peeled and sliced into very thin*
>   *rings*
> 1 *cup mayonnaise*
> *juice of 2 large lemons* } *mixed together*
>   *(5–6 tablespoons)*
> *salt*

Put a couple of cloves of garlic and a large pinch of mixed pickling spices into boiling water and then add the shrimp. Cook them just until they turn pink. Allow them to cool.

Combine the shrimp, the onion rings and the mayonnaise mixture, toss them well and refrigerate them for at least 24 hours. Add more lemon juice or salt if necessary before serving.

TOMATO ASPIC

2 *packages unflavored gelatin*
4 *cups tomato juice*
   juice of 1 lemon (2–3 tablespoons)
   salt and freshly ground pepper

GARNISH
   sliced cucumbers, green peppers, carrots, radishes

To soften the gelatin, sprinkle it over 2 cups of cold tomato juice. Heat the other 2 cups of tomato juice to the boiling point, add the gelatin mixture, the lemon juice and some salt and pepper and stir well. Pour it into a one-quart ring mold and refrigerate it until it has gelled, about three hours.

Before unmolding, run a sharp knife along the edges of the aspic to loosen it from the mold. Dip the mold briefly into a large pan of very hot water to loosen the aspic at the bottom. Place a serving plate, face down, over the mold, invert the two and unmold the aspic. (You may have to dip the mold in hot water several times before the aspic loosens, but it's best to go slowly—too much heat will make it melt.)

Fill the center of the aspic with Pickled Shrimp and Onions, p. 88, and garnish it with the raw vegetables.

This aspic can also be filled with Chicken Salad, pp. 95–96, Cole Slaw, p. 172, Eggplant Caviar, p. 72, or Green Rice, p. 121.

SATURDAY DINNER

Spicy Pork
Persian Rice
Watercress and Tomato Salad

Mocha Nut Cake

SPICY PORK

Any boned and tied pork roast can be cooked in this manner, but a loin of pork is by far the most elegant. Quantities are given for a roast which weighs 4 pounds *after boning.*

4-pound pork roast, boned and tied
2 tablespoons coarse salt ⎫
½ teaspoon dried thyme ⎪
¼ teaspoon powdered cloves ⎪
¼ teaspoon powdered cinnamon ⎬ *mixed together*
¼ teaspoon powdered nutmeg ⎪
2 bay leaves, crushed ⎪
15 peppercorns, crushed ⎭

Rub the mixed spices over every surface of the meat, and let it stand in the refrigerator for 24–36 hours.

Preheat the oven to 350° F.

Roast, uncovered, for 1½ hours, or until a meat thermometer registers 180°. Baste occasionally, at first with just a little hot water, later with the concentrated pan juices.

Remove the roast to a platter when it is done and let it stand for about 20 minutes. Skim the fat from the juices in the pan, or pour the juices into a metal container and place in the freezer for about 15 minutes until the fat is solid enough to remove easily. Deglaze the pan with a little water and the skimmed juices. Simmer for a minute or two and pour over the meat before serving.

PERSIAN RICE

This classic dish is simple to prepare but requires a good deal of cooking time and cannot be rushed. The unusual combination of buttery rice and crisp brown potatoes always comes as a pleasant surprise.

The long soaking in salted water and brief boiling time that we recommend will produce rice with a fine, firm texture. You have to remember to put the rice in to soak, but this only takes about 2 minutes and can even be done the night before if you're afraid you'll forget.

The dish can also be made with rice that has been boiled in the usual way or prepared as for a pilaf (see p. 108).

  2 *cups white rice*
  ¼ *cup salt*
  ½ *cup butter, melted*
  1 *Idaho potato, peeled and very thinly sliced*

Soak the rice and the salt in cold water to cover for at least 5 hours, or overnight.

About 2½ hours before serving, drain the rice and put the soaking water plus 2 quarts of fresh water in a large pot. Bring the water to a boil, add the rice and cook over high heat, stirring occasionally, for 5 minutes. Drain the rice and discard the water.

Cover the bottom of a large Dutch oven with some of the melted butter. Arrange the potato slices, slightly overlapping, over the entire bottom surface of the pot. Mound the rice on top of the potato slices. Pour the remaining butter over the rice. Place over very high heat for 5 minutes, then turn the heat as low as possible. Cover the pot, placing a thick terry towel between the pot and the cover so that no steam can escape. Cook without uncovering for about 2 hours.

When you are ready to serve, spoon the rice onto a platter and use a spatula to free the potato layer from the bottom of the pot. Try to keep it in one crisp piece. Tilt the pot and with the spatula flip the potatoes, brown side up, on top of the rice.

WATERCRESS AND TOMATO SALAD

15–20 cherry tomatoes, sliced in half, or 3 tomatoes, cut
        in wedges
  1–2 bunches of watercress, cut in half

DRESSING

juice of 1½ lemons
  (4–5 tablespoons)
2 cloves garlic, minced   } *mixed together*
1 teaspoon salt

Marinate the tomatoes in the dressing for 1–3 hours. Just before serving, add the watercress and toss it all vigorously.

This is a light and tangy dressing—do not add oil.

MOCHA NUT CAKE

This marvelous cake can be made in a blender in less time than it takes to prepare a commercial cake mix. It is infinitely superior.

  6 eggs
  1 cup sugar
1½ cups nutmeats (filberts, almonds, walnuts or pecans)
  3 tablespoons flour
  1 tablespoon baking powder
     pinch of salt

TOPPING

1½ cups heavy cream
¼ cup sugar
2 tablespoons cocoa ⎫
2 teaspoons powdered coffee ⎭ *mixed together*

Preheat the oven to 350° F.

Put the eggs and sugar in the blender container, cover and blend until smooth. Add the nuts and blend until fine. Add the flour, baking powder and salt and blend until well mixed.

Pour the batter into two well-buttered 8- or 9-inch layer pans and bake for 20 minutes. The cake is done when a toothpick inserted in the center comes out clean. Allow the layers to cool completely. Put on the topping no more than a few hours before serving.

TOPPING

Whip the cream until it begins to thicken, add the flavorings and continue to whip until stiff. Spread the cream between the layers and on the top and sides of the cake. Refrigerate.

SUNDAY LUNCH

Asparagus Hollandaise
Chicken Salad

·

Strawberries and Double Cream

ASPARAGUS HOLLANDAISE

Much fuss has been made over the proper way to cook asparagus, and special pots are even sold for that purpose alone. Our way is very simple and very satisfactory. There is only one rule to observe at all costs: *Do not overcook!*

Wash about 2 pounds of asparagus thoroughly, breaking off the ends at the point where they snap easily.

Bring about ½ inch of water to a rapid boil, using a skillet large enough to lay the asparagus flat in one layer. Add the asparagus, cover the pot and steam them rapidly until the thick ends of the asparagus are tender when pierced with the point of a sharp knife, about 10 minutes. Do not overcook or allow the asparagus to lose their bright color.

Put a fresh dish towel on the serving platter before transferring the asparagus to it. This will keep the asparagus warm while allowing them to drain into the towel. They should be served directly from it.

HOLLANDAISE SAUCE

Hollandaise Sauce can be tricky until you get the feel of it, but don't be intimidated. If you follow our directions carefully, you'll find it very simple to make and, since it's such a versatile sauce, you'll use it often.

4 *egg yolks*
¾ *cup (1½ sticks) butter, preferably unsalted, divided*
    in thirds
½ *lemon*
    pinch of salt

Place the egg yolks in the top of a double boiler over hot (not boiling) water and beat them vigorously with a wire whisk for a minute or two. Be sure to keep the water below the boiling point so that the egg yolks do not solidify. Add one third of the butter and continue beating as the butter melts and the sauce begins to thicken. Follow this procedure with the remaining two pieces of butter, beating each until it is absorbed and the sauce is creamy. Remove the pot from the heat and continue beating as you add a few drops of lemon juice and some salt to taste. The sauce should not separate, of course, but if it *does* there is a simple remedy: beat in a tablespoon or so of boiling water, which will bind it back together again.

The finished sauce may be kept for about an hour over warm (not hot) water. It should be served warm, not hot, and may be thinned, if necessary, by adding a little very hot water.

CHICKEN SALAD

Only once in an extremely compatible collaboration did we reach an impasse—and over chicken salad, no less. Happily, we found a simple solution. Both recipes follow.

CHICKEN SALAD (MOLLY FINN)
 5 *cups cooked chicken, cut into bite-sized pieces*
 3 *stalks celery, diced*
 6 *scallions, including green part, finely sliced*
 1 *medium cucumber, diced*
 1 *tablespoon fresh tarragon or parsley, chopped, or 1
     teaspoon dried tarragon*

DRESSING
 1 *cup* aioli, *p. 36*
     or
 3 *tablespoons olive oil*
 2 *tablespoons wine vinegar*
 ⅔ *cup mayonnaise*   *mixed together*
 2 *large cloves garlic, minced*
 1 *teaspoon salt*
     freshly ground pepper

One to two hours before serving, combine the chicken, vegetables and herbs with the dressing and mix well.

CHICKEN SALAD (JERI LABER)

- 5 cups cooked chicken, cut into bite-sized pieces
- 3 stalks celery, diced
- 1 tablespoon capers
  juice of 4 lemons
- 1 teaspoon salt
  freshly ground pepper
- 1 medium can (about 14 ounces) pineapple rings in heavy syrup, drained and cut into slivers

DRESSING

- ½ cup mayonnaise
- 2 teaspoons prepared mustard   } mixed together
- 2 teaspoons chili sauce

GARNISH

- ¼ cup almonds, blanched, slivered and toasted
- 4 hard-boiled eggs, sliced

Combine the chicken, celery, capers and seasoned lemon juice and let them stand in the refrigerator for at least an hour, stirring once or twice.

An hour or two before serving, drain any excess lemon juice from the bowl, add the drained pineapple and toss the salad with the mayonnaise dressing, adding more salt and pepper if necessary.

Just before serving, sprinkle with slivered almonds and garnish with sliced eggs.

STRAWBERRIES AND DOUBLE CREAM

It's hard to think of a way to improve strawberries and cream, but this is it—strawberries and double cream.

Wash and dry 2 pints of fresh strawberries but do not hull them. Sprinkle them with several spoonfuls of confectioners' sugar and refrigerate them while the sugar dissolves.

Arrange the strawberries on a platter around a small bowl of double cream, into which each strawberry should be dipped before eating. The double cream will be just thick enough to coat a dipped strawberry without dripping.

DOUBLE CREAM

Simmer 1 pint of heavy cream for about 30 minutes or until it is reduced by about ⅓, stirring frequently to keep it from boiling over. Cover and refrigerate the cream for at least a day before using. It will thicken a little more as it stands and should be stirred well before serving.

This sweet, thick cream may be kept, tightly covered, in the refrigerator for several weeks. It can be used as a topping for fruit desserts or as concentrated cream for cooking.

Menus for
JUNE

FRIDAY DINNER

Greek Lemon Soup
Chicken Florentine
Cherry Tomatoes

·

Kisselitza

SATURDAY LUNCH

Lemon Soup Custard
Artichokes Vinaigrette
Middle Eastern Flat Bread

·

Bananas in Yogurt

SATURDAY DINNER

Shish Kebab
Curried Rice Pilaf

·

Ginger Cream

SUNDAY LUNCH

Boeuf en Daube
French Bread

·

Kisselitza

Preparation Schedule

for

JUNE

[ALL RECIPES SERVE 6]

In Advance—Greek lemon soup seems so perfect for a June weekend that you should plan to serve it twice: light, frothy and hot on Friday night when the evenings may still be chilly, and tart and cold at Saturday's lunch. A good homemade chicken stock is absolutely essential to this soup. Whether you take the stock from your freezer or fix it a few days in advance, cook the chicken for the *Chicken Florentine* in the stock. You can assemble this dish a day ahead, if you wish, and refrigerate it until you are ready to put it in the oven. Prepare the *Kissel-itza*—a refreshing fruit stew—ahead of time, too; it will keep for a few weeks and can be frozen.

On Friday—On Friday evening, finish preparing the *Greek Lemon Soup* while the *Chicken Florentine* is baking.

On Saturday—On Saturday morning, or on Friday if you prefer, put the meat and vegetables for the *Shish Kebab* and the *Boeuf en Daube* in the marinade. You can cook the *Artichokes* early Saturday morning and serve them cold with *Vinaigrette Sauce*, or you can steam them 30 minutes before serving them hot.

On Saturday evening, put the marinated meat and vegetables on skewers and start the charcoal fire. You can then make the *Curried Rice Pilaf*. Fix the *Ginger Cream* just before dinner and leave it in the refrigerator, ready to serve, or prepare it later, while you're making coffee.

If you have time, you can fix the *Daube* and cook it for Sunday while you are threading the skewers for the shish kebab, or you can brown the meat, add the vegetables and refrigerate the uncooked stew in a casserole to be completed on Sunday.

FRIDAY DINNER

Greek Lemon Soup
Chicken Florentine
Cherry Tomatoes

•

Kisselitza

GREEK LEMON SOUP

   8 cups homemade chicken soup, p. 85 (see note)
½ *cup uncooked rice*
   4 eggs
    juice of 2 lemons (4–6 tablespoons)

Bring the soup to a boil, add the rice and simmer until the rice is cooked—about 20 minutes. Just before serving, beat the eggs until they are very light and foamy and then beat in the lemon juice and about 2 cups of the hot soup. Beat the egg–lemon mixture into the hot soup over low heat. Be careful not to boil the soup; if it boils the eggs will curdle and the soup will lose its frothy texture. Float a thin slice of lemon in each bowl and serve immediately.

This soup is equally delicious hot or cold. When it is chilled it will set into a lightly gelled custard, and will seem like a different soup entirely. To serve it this way for lunch on Saturday, you will only need to make 1½ times this recipe and use very small cups.

NOTE—*Cook 3 pounds of chicken breasts in the stock if you plan to make Chicken Florentine, p. 103.*

CHICKEN FLORENTINE

    2 ten-ounce packages chopped, frozen spinach
    2 large onions, chopped
       butter
    1 cup Parmesan cheese, freshly grated
 1 ½ cups ricotta cheese
    4 eggs
       salt and freshly ground pepper ⎫ beaten together
  ½ teaspoon nutmeg   ⎭
       3 cups cooked chicken, cut into small pieces (see note)
       bread crumbs

Preheat the oven to 400° F.

Cook or thaw the spinach and drain it in a sieve. Sauté the onions in butter until they are transparent but not browned. Squeeze the spinach as dry as possible and combine it well with the onions, cheeses and the egg mixture.

Butter a casserole or a soufflé dish. Put half the spinach mixture in the casserole, add the chicken, sprinkle with salt and pepper, and add the rest of the spinach mixture. Cover the top with bread crumbs, dot generously with butter and bake for 25–30 minutes, until the eggs have set and the top is browned.

This dish may be assembled as much as a day in advance. It can be served hot or at room temperature.

NOTE—*The chicken for this dish should be prepared while you are making the stock for Greek Lemon Soup, p. 102. One pound of uncooked chicken makes about 1 cup of diced, cooked chicken.*

KISSELITZA

This beautiful, tart, ruby-red fruit soup will always be *Kisselitza* to us—that's what it was called in the old country and that's what Anne Ratner called it when she made it for her daughters. A gallon jar of *Kisselitza* always appeared in the refrigerator during sour cherry season—to us it meant the end of school, the beginning of summer, the glorious bad manners of spitting all those cherry pits right back into your bowl.

Sour cherries are essential to this dish. Keep an eye out for fresh cherries during June and early July; they are far preferable to the canned ones. You can vary the proportions of the other fruits you use according to your preferences and what is available. You can usually buy slightly bruised fruits at greatly reduced prices, and it is fine to use them.

2 pounds sour cherries, stemmed (or 4 one-pound cans)
2 pounds sweet cherries, stemmed
4 pounds mixed plums, peaches, apricots and nectarines,
    cut in half and pitted
    sugar to taste

Put the fruit in a large pot, add 6 cups of water (or the juice from the canned cherries with enough water added to make 6 cups) and bring it to a boil. Lower the heat, cover the pot and simmer until the fruit is soft but not mushy—about 20 minutes. Remove the pot from the heat and add sugar with discretion, stirring until it is dissolved. Chill well before serving.

SATURDAY LUNCH

Lemon Soup Custard
Artichokes Vinaigrette
Middle Eastern Flat Bread

•

Bananas in Yogurt

ARTICHOKES VINAIGRETTE

Artichokes are good hot, warm or cold, with different sauces to dip the leaves in. Serve them hot with lemon butter or Hollandaise Sauce, p. 94, hot or cold with homemade mayonnaise, p. 36. For this lunch, serve them with a classic Sauce Vinaigrette.

Trim the artichokes, cutting off most of the stems and about 1 inch from the tops and removing any withered leaves. Wash them thoroughly. Bring 2–3 inches of salted water to a boil in a large pot. Place the artichokes in the water stem-end down, cover and boil briskly for 20–30 minutes or until the bottoms of the artichokes are tender when pierced with a sharp knife. Remove them from the water, invert them and allow them to drain in a colander.

SAUCE VINAIGRETTE

The best vinaigrette sauce is made with olive oil and wine vinegar. It can be seasoned with almost anything—minced garlic, chopped fresh herbs, a pinch of any dried herb, capers, a chopped shallot or a bit of chopped sweet or hot pepper, a pinch of dried mustard, etc.—and, of course, salt and freshly ground pepper.

The proportion of vinegar to oil can be varied according to taste. One part vinegar to three parts oil is a good beginning. Beat the oil and vinegar together thoroughly with a fork and taste; then add vinegar to make it sharper, oil for a blander sauce.

For 6 artichokes you will need a cup of Sauce Vinaigrette.

¼ *cup wine vinegar*
¾ *cup olive oil*
¼ *teaspoon dry mustard*
  salt and freshly ground pepper

Beat the sauce well with a fork and serve a small cup of it with each artichoke.

BANANAS IN YOGURT

4 *large bananas*
½ *fresh pineapple, diced (optional) (see note)*
2 *tablespoons brown sugar* ⎫
1 *cup yogurt* ⎭ *mixed together*

Combine the bananas and the pineapple and toss them lightly in the sweetened yogurt.

NOTE—*Use the rest of the pineapple in Shish Kebab, p. 107.*

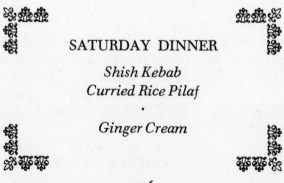

SATURDAY DINNER

Shish Kebab
Curried Rice Pilaf

·

Ginger Cream

SHISH KEBAB

From one herb-scented wine marinade come two very distinct and distinctive dinners: a sizzling shish kebab and a succulent stew—Boeuf en Daube, p. 110. It's hard to believe that it's only the way they're cooked that makes them so different from each other.

TO BE MARINATED (see note)
> 3 *pounds beef, cut into 1½-inch cubes*
> 1 *pound small white onions, peeled*
> ½ *pound mushrooms, caps only (save the stems for the*
> > *Boeuf en Daube, p. 110)*
> 3 *small zucchini, cut in thick slices*

MARINADE
> 1½ *cups dry red wine*
> ½ *cup olive oil*
> 3 *cloves garlic, minced*
> 1 *teaspoon basil*   } *mixed together*
> 1 *teaspoon oregano*
> 1 *bay leaf*
> 1 *tablespoon salt*
> *freshly ground pepper*

> 2 *green peppers, seeded and cut up*
> 12 *cherry tomatoes (or 3 medium tomatoes cut in*
> > *wedges)*
> ½ *fresh pineapple, cut in small pieces (optional) (see*
> > *note)*
> > *about ½ pound sliced bacon, cut into squares*

Put the meat, onions, mushrooms and zucchini in a large pan and pour the marinade over them. Refrigerate, covered, for up to 24 hours, stirring occasionally.

Thread the meat and vegetables (and pineapple, if used), on 12 short or 6 long skewers, putting a square of bacon between every 3 or 4 pieces and dividing the other ingredients evenly. Figure on about 6 pieces of meat for each serving and prepare an extra skewer or two of only vegetables if they are left.

Cook over a charcoal fire until the meat is done the way you like it. Because it has been marinated, it will cook very rapidly, so take care not to overcook it.

NOTE—*Double the quantities of the ingredients to be marinated and add another cup of wine to the marinade if you are also preparing* Boeuf en Daube, *p. 110.*

Add the rest of the pineapple to Bananas in Yogurt, p. 106.

CURRIED RICE PILAF

2 small onions, diced
2 small apples, peeled, cored and diced
  butter
1½ cups rice
3 cups chicken broth, heated to
    boiling point
  approximately 2 teaspoons curry   } mixed together
    powder
  salt and freshly ground pepper
2 tablespoons dried currants (or raisins)

Sauté the onions and apples in butter in a large skillet until they are transparent. Add the rice and brown it for a few minutes, using more butter if necessary and stirring constantly to prevent it from burning. Add the seasoned chicken broth (watch out for a blast of steam) and the currants, stir, cover and cook over very low heat without stirring again until the rice is done and the liquid is absorbed, about 20 minutes.

The rice may be reheated in the same pan or in a buttered dish in a moderate oven.

GINGER CREAM

You can make and serve this dessert—whipped cream with a little flavoring—in about five minutes. Serve very tiny portions. No one will be able to guess what it is.

> 1 *cup heavy cream*
> 1 *tablespoon honey*
> 1–2 *tablespoons rum*
> 1 *heaping tablespoon chopped crystallized ginger*

Beat the cream. When it begins to thicken, beat in the honey and the rum and continue to beat until the cream stands in soft peaks. Fold in the chopped ginger. Spoon the cream evenly into 6 demitasse cups or small wine glasses. Top each with a piece of ginger. Refrigerate the cream until you are ready to serve it.

This dessert lends itself to infinite variations. A glance through your baking and bar supplies will inspire you. Some combinations we like: brown sugar, almond extract and chopped almonds; Grand Marnier and grated orange rind; powdered coffee, cocoa, sugar and chopped walnuts; brandy and chopped candied fruits.

SUNDAY LUNCH

Boeuf en Daube
French Bread

•

Kisselitza

BOEUF EN DAUBE

The basic ingredients for this stew are almost the same as those for Shish Kebab, p. 107. If you are preparing both dishes for the same weekend, marinate all the ingredients together.

TO BE MARINATED

   3 *pounds beef, cut into 1½-inch cubes*
   1 *pound small white onions, peeled*
  ½ *pound mushrooms*
   3 *small zucchini, cut in thick slices*

MARINADE (see note)

 1½ *cups dry red wine*
  ½ *cup olive oil*
   3 *cloves garlic, minced*
   1 *teaspoon basil*
   1 *teaspoon oregano*   }   *mixed together*
   1 *bay leaf*
   1 *tablespoon salt*

   3 *slices bacon, cut into small pieces*

PERSILLADE

  ½ *cup chopped parsley*
   2 *medium cloves garlic, minced*
 1–2 *tablespoons capers*   }   *mixed together*
   3 *anchovies, chopped* (optional)

Preheat the oven to 275° F.

Marinate the meat for at least 6 hours. You can add the vegetables to the marinade with the meat or several hours later if you wish. Remove the meat from the marinade and pat it as dry as possible with paper towels. Sauté the bacon pieces in a large casserole until they are browned but not quite crisp. Brown the meat on all sides in the bacon fat. Take the vegetables out of the marinade and stir them into the meat. [Any cooked, leftover Shish Kebab can be added to the stewpot at this point.] Cover the casserole and cook the *Daube* in the oven for 1–1½ hours, until the meat is tender enough to cut with a fork. Just before serving, stir in the *persillade* and season with salt and pepper if necessary.

You may prepare this dish in advance and reheat it, but do not add the *persillade* until just before serving.

NOTE—*If you are marinating the ingredients for the Shish Kebab, p. 107, together with the ingredients for the* Daube, *add another cup of wine to the marinade.*

Menus for
JULY

FRIDAY DINNER

Savory Meat Pie
Green Beans Vinaigrette

·

Melon Mélange

SATURDAY LUNCH

Vichysquash
Sardines, Etc.

·

Fruit and Cheese

SATURDAY DINNER

Lemon Chicken
Cucumbers in Sour Cream
Green Rice

·

Almond Mousse au Chocolat

SUNDAY LUNCH

Sunday Smorgasbord:
Cold Meat Pie
Chicken
Cucumber Salad
Green Rice

·

Clafoutis

Preparation Schedule

for

JULY

Summer meals should be easy to fix, and these are. There is nothing that has to be done in advance for this July weekend. All the dishes can be prepared during the cool part of the day and need little or no tending while they are cooking.

On Friday—It will take time to assemble the *Savory Meat Pie* for Friday's dinner, but you can do it in several stages, or bake it hours in advance and reheat it or serve it at room temperature. Prepare the *Green Beans Vinaigrette* and the *Melon Mélange* before putting the pie in to bake or reheat.

On Friday or Saturday—*Vichysquash*, the soup for Saturday's lunch, and the *Green Rice* and *Almond Mousse au Chocolat* for Saturday's dinner may all be done a day ahead or, if it's more convenient, on Saturday morning. If you wait until Saturday morning, make the soup first so it has time to chill before lunch.

On Saturday—Set the *Lemon Chicken* to marinate some time Saturday afternoon. If you prepare the *Cucumbers in Sour Cream* at the same time, your dinner will be complete; all you'll have to do is put the chicken in the oven when it's time to cook it.

On Sunday—On Sunday, make the *Clafoutis* about an hour before lunch. The *Sunday Smorgasbord* will be ready and waiting in the refrigerator.

FRIDAY DINNER

Savory Meat Pie
Green Beans Vinaigrette

·

Melon Mélange

SAVORY MEAT PIE

CRUST (see note)

¾ cup butter, cut into small pieces
2 cups flour ⎱
pinch of salt ⎰ mixed together
4–6 tablespoons sour cream or enough to bind the dough

FILLING (see note)

3 hard-boiled eggs, chopped
2 large onions, chopped
   butter or chicken fat
2 pounds ground beef
2 teaspoons salt and lots of freshly ground pepper
1½ tablespoons fresh savory (or parsley), chopped, or 1
   teaspoon dried savory
¾ cup Swiss cheese, coarsely grated

1 egg, beaten

Prepare the pie dough by working the butter into the flour and salt, using a pastry blender, a fork or your fingers, until it has the consistency of meal. Stir in the sour cream with a fork and work the dough into a ball. Refrigerate it while you prepare the filling.

Set the eggs to boil. Sauté the onions in butter or chicken fat until they are lightly browned. While they are cooking, grate the cheese. Remove the onions to a large bowl, add the meat to the pan and cook it, breaking it up with a fork, until it is cooked but not dry. While the meat is cooking, chop the eggs and add them to the bowl. Remove the meat from the pan with a slotted spoon, put it in the bowl with the onions and the eggs, add the seasonings and combine it all thoroughly. Make sure the meat mixture is well seasoned, then stir in the cheese.

Preheat the oven to 375° F.

Line a 10- or 11-inch pie plate with half the pastry and spoon in the filling. Roll out the rest of the dough and cover the pie, pressing the edges together with the back of a fork. Brush the top with the beaten egg, prick it all over to allow the air to escape and bake it in the lower part of the oven for about 40 minutes or until the pie is golden brown.

NOTE—*If you plan to include this meat pie in a Sunday Smorgasbord, double the pie crust recipe and bake the pie in a 9- by 13-inch pan. You will not need to double the filling, since the smorgasbord menu assumes small portions of a variety of dishes. For the filling use 3 onions, 3½ pounds of beef, 5 eggs, 3 teaspoons salt, 2 tablespoons fresh savory and 1 cup of grated Swiss cheese. The meat pie for the smorgasbord may be reheated in a slow oven or served at room temperature with sour cream and chopped chives.*

GREEN BEANS VINAIGRETTE

    2 *pounds green beans*
4–5 *sprigs fresh thyme, or ½ teaspoon dried*
        salt

VINAIGRETTE SAUCE
  ½ *cup olive oil*
    3 *tablespoons white wine vinegar*   } *beaten together with a fork*
        salt and freshly ground pepper

Choose fresh beans that snap when you bend them. Wash them and break off the ends.

Cover the bottom of a pot with about an inch of water, put in the thyme and some salt and bring the water to a rapid boil. Add the beans, cover the pot and cook the beans briskly until they are just tender. As with all fresh vegetables, be careful not to overcook the beans. They should be a little crisp, not soggy, and keep their fresh color. Drain them and add the vinaigrette sauce. Toss them from time to time as they cool. Serve them at room temperature.

MELON MÉLANGE

The cool appearance of this beautiful blue and green dessert will be enhanced if you serve it in a frosted glass bowl.

    1 *large or 2 small honeydew melons*
    2 *tablespoons sugar*
       juice of 1 orange (only fresh orange juice will do)
    1 *pint blueberries*

Cut the melon into bite-sized chunks. Sprinkle with sugar and orange juice. Add the blueberries. Chill in a serving bowl, stirring occasionally so that all the melon is flavored with the juice.

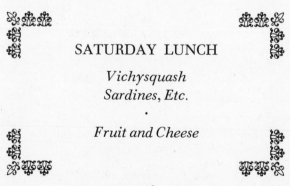

SATURDAY LUNCH

Vichysquash
Sardines, Etc.

.

Fruit and Cheese

VICHYSQUASH

This is a lovely, pale, delicate summer soup. Freeze the puree and it will be a lovely winter soup, too.

1 medium onion, peeled and sliced
*   butter*
6 medium summer (yellow) squash, sliced
½ cup chicken broth
*   salt and freshly ground pepper*
1 cup milk or light cream
*   chopped chives*

Sauté the onion in butter in a large pan. When it is wilted but not brown, add the squash and the broth. Cover and cook briskly until the squash is very tender, about 15 minutes. Puree the squash with the cooking liquid in a blender or put it all through a food mill. Season the soup with salt and pepper. Chill, add the milk or cream and serve it cold, sprinkled with chives.

SARDINES, ETC.

Arrange several different kinds of sardines on a platter and surround them with lemon wedges, sliced tomatoes and Bermuda onion rings. Serve them with pumpernickel and butter.

SATURDAY DINNER

Lemon Chicken
Cucumbers in Sour Cream
Green Rice

·

Almond Mousse au Chocolat

LEMON CHICKEN

2 *chickens, cut into small serving pieces* (see note)

MARINADE
1 *cup olive oil*
½ *cup lemon juice* (*3 lemons*)
2 *tablespoons dried oregano* ⎱ *mixed together*
3 *cloves garlic, minced*
salt and freshly ground pepper ⎰

Put the chicken in a large baking pan, pour the marinade over it and let it stand for at least 2 hours, turning the chicken occasionally.
Preheat the oven to 350° F.
Turn the chicken skin-side down in the marinade and roast it in the oven for 30–40 minutes, until the chicken is just done. Turn the chicken, place it under the broiler and broil it until the skin is crisp and brown.
The chicken can be kept in a 200° F. oven for about an hour before serving. Pour the pan juices over the chicken when you serve it.
If you wish, you may grill the chicken over a charcoal fire. Place the marinated chicken on heavy foil which has been perforated every inch or so and baste it with the marinade as it cooks. The charcoal will flavor the chicken without making it dry.

NOTE—*Add an extra chicken if you plan to include this dish in a Sunday Smorgasbord.*

CUCUMBERS IN SOUR CREAM

6 *medium cucumbers, peeled and very thinly sliced* (see note)

DRESSING
¾ *cup sour cream*
2 *tablespoons vinegar*
1 *tablespoon chives, chopped* ⎱ *mixed together*
salt and freshly ground pepper ⎰

The vinegar will make this sour cream dressing a little frothy. Toss the cucumbers in it and chill well.

NOTE—*Prepare a little extra for a Sunday Smorgasbord.*

GREEN RICE

For variety, try this herb dressing with cracked wheat (bulghur), millet, barley or any of the other grains that are now so easily available in most markets.

    2 cups white or brown rice (or some other grain) (see note)

DRESSING
*⅔ cup olive oil
   juice of 2 lemons (4–6 tablespoons)
 2 tablespoons chives, chopped
 2 tablespoons parsley, chopped
 2 tablespoons basil, chopped
 2 teaspoons marjoram, chopped
   salt and freshly ground pepper*   } *mixed together*

Cook the rice, drain it and let it cool. Toss it with the dressing. Serve it at room temperature.

NOTE—*If you plan to serve this rice as part of a Sunday Smorgasbord, cook another cup of rice and increase the dressing accordingly.*

ALMOND MOUSSE AU CHOCOLAT

   *1 envelope gelatin
   3 squares unsweetened chocolate
 ½ cup milk
 ½ cup sugar
   1 pint heavy cream
 ¼ teaspoon almond extract
 ½ cup blanched almonds, chopped*

grated sweet chocolate
toasted almonds

Soak the gelatin in ¼ cup of cold water to soften it. Melt the chocolate in the milk over boiling water. Add the sugar, and stir the mixture until it is thoroughly blended. Add the gelatin, and continue to stir until it is completely dissolved. Let it cool. (This may be hastened by putting the pot into cold water, stirring frequently to prevent gelling around the edges.)

Whip the cream until it stands in soft peaks. Stir the almond extract and the chopped almonds into the cooled chocolate, and then fold in the whipped cream. Pour it into an attractive serving bowl and let it set in the refrigerator for at least two hours. Decorate with grated chocolate or toasted almonds before serving. You can make this dessert a day in advance, if you wish.

SUNDAY LUNCH

Sunday Smorgasbord:
  Cold Meat Pie
  Chicken
  Cucumber Salad
  Green Rice

·

Clafoutis

SUNDAY SMORGASBORD

We have found that a Sunday buffet at the end of the weekend often becomes a pleasantly nostalgic review of meals that have gone before. Nobody minds eating good things twice, especially when they are combined in new and interesting ways. Sometimes this happens by accident; sometimes we plan a weekend with this specifically in mind, as we have done here:

Cold Meat Pie with Sour Cream and Chives (p. 116)
Lemon Chicken (p. 120)
Cucumber Salad (p. 120)
Green Rice (p. 121)
Sliced Tomatoes
Italian Breadsticks

Clafoutis (see below)

CLAFOUTIS

Clafoutis is neither a custard nor a pancake, but is a little bit like each. Try it with different kinds of fruit, or with a mixture of several. It's beautiful to look at and simple to make.

3 cups fruit (pitted cherries, seedless grapes, berries, or
    sliced peaches, plums, pears or apples)
¼ cup sugar

BATTER
1 cup milk
3 eggs
½ cup flour
1 tablespoon sugar
2 teaspoons vanilla

Preheat the oven to 350° F.

Butter an 11-inch pie plate or a medium-sized shallow baking dish. Place the fruit in the bottom of the pan and sprinkle with the sugar.

Mix the batter in a blender or beat it very well with a beater. Pour it over the fruit and bake it for about one-half hour. Serve the *Clafoutis* warm (remove it from the oven when you sit down to dinner).

Menus for
AUGUST

FRIDAY DINNER

Hamburgers on Rye with
Scallion Butter
Creamed Summer Squash
Corn-on-the-Cob

•

Applesauce Brownies

SATURDAY LUNCH

Cottage Cheese Lunch:
Sour Cream and Cottage Cheese
Salmon
Raw Vegetables and Herbs
Rolls and Bagels

·

Blueberries

SATURDAY DINNER

Cucumber Ice
Striped Bass in White Wine
New Potatoes

·

Watermelon

SUNDAY LUNCH

Tossed Tuna Salad
Pepperoni Potato Salad

·

Plum Cake

Preparation Schedule

for

AUGUST

[ALL RECIPES SERVE 6]

Since the recipes for this August weekend make such good use of all the wonderful fruits and vegetables that are in season, we suggest a visit to the best market or farm stand you know—unless you're lucky enough to have these good things growing in your own garden.

This may well be the hottest weekend of the year, but you won't have to be in the kitchen when the oven is going. We've chosen the two easiest cakes we know—you don't even need a beater. Each can be assembled in about ten minutes, and they are very, very good.

In Advance—It is not absolutely necessary to do anything in advance for this weekend, but you might want to make the *Applesauce Brownies* a day or two ahead.

On Friday—Before you light the outdoor fire on Friday, start heating a big pot of water for the *Corn* and begin cooking the *Summer Squash*. The rest of the meal can be prepared in the time it takes the charcoal to get hot. If you put the corn in the boiling water right after you put the *Hamburgers* on the grill and then make the *Scallion Butter*, everything should be ready at about the same time. Not that it really matters; we often serve corn as a separate course, before or after the main dish.

On Saturday—On Saturday morning you can finish your weekend's cooking in a busy hour or two, depending on how much help you can get from guests and older children. Most of the work involves cutting up vegetables for the *Cottage Cheese Lunch*, for the *Cucumber Ice*, for the *Striped Bass* and for the

Potato Salad. Make the *Cucumber Ice* and wrap the chopped herbs and vegetables in foil packages, setting aside some of the chopped onion for the potato and tuna salads. Get the *Striped Bass in White Wine* all ready for cooking in a covered baking dish and refrigerate it until dinner time. You should now be able to breeze through the rest of the weekend with the efficiency of a well-organized restaurant chef.

On Sunday—If you haven't made the *Plum Cake* before Sunday—and there's no reason why you should—fix the *Tossed Tuna Salad* and the *Pepperoni Potato Salad* first and let them stand at room temperature while the cake is baking.

FRIDAY DINNER

Hamburgers on Rye with Scallion Butter
Creamed Summer Squash
Corn-on-the-Cob

·

Applesauce Brownies

HAMBURGERS ON RYE WITH SCALLION BUTTER

> 3 *pounds ground beef, formed into 12 patties*
> *coarsely ground or cracked black pepper*
> 2 *bunches scallions, trimmed into 6-inch lengths (save the*
> *tops for Scallion Butter)*
>
> SCALLION BUTTER (mash all ingredients together)
> 4 *tablespoons butter, softened*
> 1 *tablespoon scallion tops, finely chopped*
> 1 *clove garlic, minced*

1 *tablespoon parsley, finely chopped*
   squeeze of lemon juice
   salt
   rye bread

These are best charcoal-broiled. While the coals are heating, press plenty of pepper into the surfaces of the patties and prepare the scallion butter. Grill the hamburgers. While they are cooking, toast the bread and butter it with the scallion butter. Put the hamburgers on the buttered toast and garnish with scallions.

CREAMED SUMMER SQUASH

6 *medium yellow summer squash, sliced* (see note)
   butter
   salt and freshly ground pepper
   sour cream
   caraway seeds

Put a little salted water in a large skillet, add the squash, cover and steam until it is soft. [Set aside about 3 cups of cooked squash at this point if you are also preparing Pepperoni Potato Salad.] Pour off the liquid and chop or mash the squash with some butter, salt and pepper.

Just before serving, reheat the squash if necessary and stir in a pinch of caraway seeds and a few tablespoons of sour cream.

NOTE—*Cook 3 more squash if you plan to make* Pepperoni Potato Salad, *p. 134.*

CORN-ON-THE-COB

Shuck 12 ears of fresh corn as close to cooking time as possible. Half fill a large pot with water and allow up to 30 minutes to bring the water to a boil. Put in the corn, cover and bring the water back to a boil. Let the water boil rapidly for three minutes and the corn will be ready.

APPLESAUCE BROWNIES

These are especially good when made with tart, homemade applesauce (p. 156), if you have some in your freezer.

½ cup butter
2 ounces unsweetened chocolate
1 cup sugar
2 eggs, well beaten
½ cup applesauce
1 teaspoon vanilla
1 cup flour
½ teaspoon baking powder
¼ teaspoon baking soda
¼ teaspoon salt
½ cup chopped nuts (optional)

Preheat the oven to 375° F.

Melt the butter and chocolate together over hot water. Remove from the heat and stir in the sugar, eggs, applesauce and vanilla. Add the dry ingredients and stir well. Fold in the chopped nuts, if you wish.

Bake in a buttered 8-inch-square pan for 35–40 minutes.

SATURDAY LUNCH

Cottage Cheese Lunch:
  Sour Cream and Cottage Cheese
  Salmon
  Raw Vegetables and Herbs
  Rolls and Bagels

•

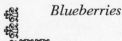

  Blueberries

COTTAGE CHEESE LUNCH

There's plenty of room for improvisation for both host and guest in this do-it-yourself lunch.

Surround bowls of cottage cheese and sour cream with small dishes or mounds of diced cucumbers, chopped Bermuda onions, diced red or green peppers, tomato wedges, sliced radishes, caraway seeds, and chopped parsley, chives and other fresh herbs.

Canned salmon sprinkled with vinegar and chopped onion, fresh rolls and bagels with sweet butter and a bowl of blueberries make this a complete and delightful meal.

SATURDAY DINNER

Cucumber Ice
Striped Bass in White Wine
New Potatoes

·

Watermelon

CUCUMBER ICE

You never tasted cucumbers half as cool as these.

¼ cup white or cider vinegar
¾ cup water
1 teaspoon salt
2 teaspoons sugar } *mixed together*

6 medium or 8 small cucumbers, peeled and cut into chunks

½ *a small onion, peeled and cut up*

fresh dill, finely chopped

Pour half the liquid mixture into the container of an electric blender. Gradually add the cucumbers and onion and puree them, emptying the container and adding more liquid and vegetables until all have been used. Season with more salt or sugar if necessary.

About 30–40 minutes before serving, pour the puree into a metal bowl and put it in the freezer. When you are ready to serve it, scrape the frozen portions from the bottom and sides of the bowl and mash them into the liquid in the center to form a slushy sherbet. Serve immediately, sprinkled with chopped dill.

If you want to save time, follow this recipe but use only ¼ cup of water in the vinegar mixture. Just before serving, add 4 or 5 ice cubes to the puree in the blender and whirl until they disappear. The cucumber ice won't solidify, but it will be very, very cold.

STRIPED BASS IN WHITE WINE

This whole baked fish is an impressive sight, even without the addition of shellfish, which we have made optional depending on expense and availability. Any fish in season may be cooked in this manner, and any combination of shellfish may be added at the end.

1 *six-pound striped bass or sea trout, whole and prepared*
   for stuffing with center bone removed (or 2 three-
   pound fish)
   salt and freshly ground pepper
2 *lemons, thinly sliced*
½ *cup scallions, thinly sliced*
½ *cup parsley, chopped*
1 *cup dry white wine*
½ *cup olive oil*
   cherry tomatoes (optional)
   clams or mussels (optional)
   raw shrimp, peeled, washed and shelled (optional)
   scallops (optional)

2 *pounds new potatoes* (see note)
  melted butter
  chopped dill

Preheat the oven to 375° F.

Sprinkle the inside of the fish with salt and pepper and fill the cavity with one sliced lemon and half of the scallions and parsley. Place the fish in a large baking pan and pour the wine and the oil over it. Sprinkle it with salt and pepper, arrange the remaining lemon slices along the length of the fish and sprinkle the remaining parsley and scallions over all. Cover the pan tightly with foil and bake for 30–40 minutes (20–30 minutes if the fish are small).

Set a pot of water to boil as soon as the fish is in the oven. Scrub the potatoes and cook them in the boiling water for about 20 minutes, until they are fork tender but still firm. [Set aside the extra potatoes you have cooked for the Pepperoni Potato Salad.] Toss the potatoes in melted butter and chopped dill.

If you plan to add shellfish and/or tomatoes to the fish, do so 10–15 minutes before the cooking is completed. Remove the foil and surround the fish with the clams or mussels, shrimp, scallops and tomatoes, or any combination you wish. Replace the foil and continue to bake until the clam or mussel shells have opened.

NOTE—*Boil 2 extra pounds of potatoes if you plan to make* Pepperoni Potato Salad, *p. 134.*

SUNDAY LUNCH

Tossed Tuna Salad
Pepperoni Potato Salad

·

Plum Cake

TOSSED TUNA SALAD

DRESSING

⅔ cup olive oil
    juice of 2 lemons (4–6 tablespoons)
2 cloves garlic, minced   } mixed together
1 teaspoon oregano or marjoram
1 teaspoon salt
    freshly ground pepper

2 ten-ounce cans or 3 seven-ounce cans tunafish, drained
    and broken into chunks
1 one-pound can small white beans, washed in cold water
    and drained (optional)
1 sweet red onion, diced
1 pound escarole, washed and cut up as for salad

Put the tunafish, the beans and the onion in a large salad bowl, pour the dressing over them, stir and allow them to marinate for at least ½ hour. Just before serving, add the escarole and toss thoroughly.

PEPPERONI POTATO SALAD

This salad originated as a response to unexpected guests. Its ingredients were determined by what happened to be in the refrigerator, but the finished dish had such a good combination of colors, tastes and textures that we have since prepared it many times. The quantities here are just for guidance—they may be varied according to your taste and whatever you happen to have on hand. Although the menus for this weekend anticipate a Sunday supply of cooked squash and potatoes, this salad is certainly worth preparing from scratch.

    approximately 2 pounds (4 cups) cold, cooked potatoes,
      peeled and diced
    approximately 1½ pounds (2½–3 cups) cold, cooked
      summer squash, diced

2 large tomatoes, cut into bite-sized chunks
½ red or Bermuda onion, diced
¾ cup sour cream
   lots of salt and freshly ground pepper
½ pound pepperoni, thinly sliced
   black olives

Combine all the ingredients, except for the pepperoni and olives, and allow them to stand at room temperature for an hour before serving. Garnish with the pepperoni and olives.

PLUM CAKE

This cake is simple to make and provides a perfect foil for any kind of fruit. You may even use canned plums or apricots when fresh fruit is not in season.

½ cup butter, softened
1¼ cups flour
 1 teaspoon baking powder
¼ teaspoon salt   } mixed together
 2 tablespoons sugar
 2 egg yolks, beaten with 2 tablespoons milk
 3 cups fresh plums, about 1½ pounds sliced and pitted

TOPPING
 2 tablespoons sugar
½ teaspoon cinnamon   } mixed together
   butter

Preheat the oven to 350° F.

Cream the butter until it is light and fluffy. Gradually add the dry ingredients and blend them in thoroughly. Add the egg yolks and mix them in well. Using your fingers, press the dough evenly into an ungreased 8- or 9-inch pan. Cover it with even rows of sliced plums.

Sprinkle the plums with the sugar and cinnamon mixture, using additional sugar if the fruit is especially tart. Dot generously with butter and bake for 35–40 minutes.

Serve warm or cool.

Menus for
SEPTEMBER

FRIDAY DINNER

Spaghetti alla Carbonara
Sliced Tomatoes with Basil
Italian Bread

·

Fruit Salad

SATURDAY LUNCH

Chunky Tomato Soup
Spinach Salad
Hot Garlic or Herb Bread
Ricotta Cheese

SATURDAY DINNER

Charcoal-broiled Steak
Sautéed Zucchini
Stuffed Tomatoes
Baked Eggplant
·
Charcoal-broiled Peaches

SUNDAY LUNCH

Green Pepper Antipasto
Cold Tomato Soup Puree
Sliced Steak Sandwiches
·
Amaretti

Preparation Schedule

for

SEPTEMBER

[ALL RECIPES SERVE 6]

You don't have to give this weekend a thought until it's time to go to the market or to your garden for tomatoes. You'll need plenty of them and they are now at their peak. If you want to do something in advance, you can fix the tomato soup a few days ahead and the fruit salad early on Friday. But you can easily make the soup—and everything else—once the weekend has begun.

On Friday—The *Spaghetti alla Carbonara* for Friday's dinner *must* be made at the last minute. If it's convenient, fry some extra bacon and boil some eggs for Saturday's *Spinach Salad* while you're preparing the Carbonara Sauce. Set aside the extra egg whites from the Carbonara Sauce for Sunday's dessert. If you haven't made the *Fruit Salad* in advance, fix it and put it in the refrigerator before you begin preparing the pasta.

On Saturday—Some time on Saturday, get the *Eggplant* in the oven, stuff the *Tomatoes* and put them in the same oven to bake. You can do this early in the day, while you are cooking the *Tomato Soup*, unless you've made it in advance. When the vegetables are done, take them out and bake the *Amaretti* for Sunday. Your weekend cooking will then be just about done, especially if you can get somebody else to tend the grill at dinner time. Cook the *Zucchini* while the *Steak* is broiling; prepare the *Peaches* but don't put them on the grill until everyone has finished the main course.

Since the meals for this weekend use seasonal fruits and vegetables which are relatively inexpensive, you should buy plenty of steak and plan to have some left for sandwiches on Sunday.

FRIDAY DINNER

Spaghetti alla Carbonara
Sliced Tomatoes with Basil
Italian Bread

·

Fruit Salad

SPAGHETTI ALLA CARBONARA

The great virtue of this meal, in addition to its being so *good*, is that it can be prepared quickly and at a moment's notice from ingredients that are generally at hand. Try to avoid that insipid concoction that is sold in jars as "grated Parmesan cheese"—it bears no resemblance to the real thing, nor can we think of a recipe in which it would be an acceptable substitute. A piece of Parmesan cheese will keep almost indefinitely in the refrigerator and be there when you need it.

> 1 *pound bacon*
> 1½ *pounds spaghetti*
> ¼ *cup butter, softened*

SAUCE

> 3 *eggs, lightly beaten*
> 3 *egg yolks, lightly beaten* (see note)
> ½ *cup cream or milk*
> ½ *cup Parmesan cheese, freshly grated*
> *salt and freshly ground pepper*

mixed together

> *about ½ cup Parmesan cheese, freshly grated*

Fry the bacon until it is crisp, drain it and break it into bite-sized pieces.

Cook the pasta in boiling, salted water until it is just done. Drain it and rinse it quickly with very hot water. Put the pasta back in the pot and toss it with the softened butter over very low heat until the butter has melted. Add the bacon and remove the pot from the heat. Pour the sauce over the pasta and toss it quickly, until the pasta is well coated. The heat of the pasta will cook and thicken the sauce slightly. Serve immediately and pass around more Parmesan cheese, salt and a pepper mill.

NOTE—*Reserve the whites for* Amaretti, *p. 149.*

SLICED TOMATOES WITH BASIL

Slice 4 to 6 large ripe tomatoes. Arrange them on a platter and sprinkle them with fresh, chopped basil. If you don't have fresh basil, just put the tomatoes in a basket with a small, sharp knife. September tomatoes need little adornment.

FRUIT SALAD

Even second-rate fruit can be made into a first-rate fruit salad. But for a superlative salad, use the best fruit.

Things to remember when making fruit salad:

- Aim for contrast in flavors, textures and colors, whether you are using 2 different fruits or 10.
- Put in a bit of something unexpected—a few nuts, some cut-up dried fruit, a little chopped fresh or candied orange rind or ginger, a sprinkling of toasted coconut.
- Sweeten the fruit with something that tastes good—honey, brown sugar, a sweet wine or liqueur.
- To turn a fruit salad into a fancy dessert, make a sauce for it. A simple one is a package of frozen raspberries or strawberries pureed in the blender. For something more elegant and unusual, beat 2 or 3 egg yolks with ¼ cup of sugar and ¼ cup of brandy, kirsch or whiskey until the sugar is completely dissolved and the sauce is thick and light.

SATURDAY LUNCH

Chunky Tomato Soup
Spinach Salad
Hot Garlic or Herb Bread
Ricotta Cheese

CHUNKY TOMATO SOUP

We give a hot and a cold version of this soup, similar to each other yet different enough to be served both ways during the same weekend. This is the hot soup—a substantial one with pieces of tomato and onion in it. The cold soup, p. 149, is a subtle and elegant puree. Both are splendid.

NOTE—Double this recipe if you plan to serve *Cold Tomato Soup Puree*, p. 149.

>   3 *tablespoons butter*
>   2 *tablespoons olive oil*
>   1 *large Bermuda onion, very thinly sliced*
>   1 *tablespoon fresh basil, chopped, or 1 teaspoon dried*
> ½ *teaspoon thyme*
>   *salt (about 1–1½ teaspoons) and freshly ground*
>   *pepper*
> 6–8 *large tomatoes, cut up*
>   *about 3 cups chicken broth*
>   *about 1 teaspoon sugar*

Melt the butter and oil in a large pot. Add the onion, basil, thyme, salt and pepper and cook the onion until it is transparent but not brown. Add the tomatoes and simmer them, stirring occasionally, for about ½ hour. Stir in the broth and continue to simmer everything for about 30 minutes more, stirring frequently and tasting for seasonings. Add a little sugar if necessary to cut the acidity of the tomatoes. Serve hot with Croutons.

CROUTONS

Freshly made croutons are vastly superior to packaged ones, and they're very easy to make.

6 slices white bread
  butter (or olive oil and 2 cloves garlic, cut in half)

Preheat the oven to 350° F.

Stack the slices of bread and cut them into ½-inch cubes. Melt enough butter to cover the bottom of a shallow, oven-proof pan (or heat the olive oil with the garlic, if you prefer garlic croutons), quickly toss the bread cubes in the butter and then toast them in the oven for 15–20 minutes, shaking the pan once or twice so the croutons can brown evenly.

SPINACH SALAD

1 pound (or 1 package) fresh spinach, washed, dried and
  cut up as for salad
½ pound sliced bacon, fried until crisp and crumbled into
  small pieces
3 eggs, hard-boiled and coarsely chopped
½ pound mushrooms, washed and sliced

DRESSING
¼ cup olive oil
¼ cup wine vinegar
1 teaspoon white horseradish
1 teaspoon chili sauce   } *mixed together*
½ teaspoon prepared mustard
  salt and freshly ground pepper

Combine the spinach, bacon, eggs and mushrooms in a salad bowl. Toss well in the dressing just before serving.

143

HOT GARLIC OR HERB BREAD

1 *loaf French bread*

GARLIC BUTTER
½ *cup softened butter*
2 *cloves garlic, minced and mashed into the butter*

HERB BUTTER
½ *cup softened butter*
2 *tablespoons chopped fresh herbs, mixed into the butter*

Preheat the oven to 325° F.

Split a loaf of French or Italian bread lengthwise and spread both cut surfaces with garlic butter or with herb butter. Lay the halves, buttered side up, on foil, and heat until the butter has melted and the bread is crisp, about 10 to 15 minutes.

SATURDAY DINNER
Charcoal-broiled Steak
Sautéed Zucchini
Stuffed Tomatoes
Baked Eggplant

·

Charcoal-broiled Peaches

CHARCOAL-BROILED STEAK

There is nothing better than a 2-inch-thick sirloin steak, charcoal-broiled. But a thick, well-marbled round or shoulder steak (London broil) is much cheaper and still very good. Sliced thin, at a sharp angle, it should be very tender.

Allow 3 pounds of meat for 6 people, 4½ pounds if you plan to serve steak sandwiches on Sunday. Let the meat come to room temperature, then cook it over hot coals until it is as rare or as well-cooked as you want it.

SAUTÉED ZUCCHINI

   olive oil
2 *scallions, including green part, chopped*
6 *medium zucchini, sliced* (see note)
   chopped parsley

Cover the bottom of a large frying pan with a film of olive oil. When the oil is hot, add the scallions and cook them briefly. Add the zucchini and sauté gently, turning frequently, until it is just tender, about 20 minutes. Sprinkle with salt, pepper and a generous amount of chopped parsley.

This is good cold, too, with a squeeze of lemon juice or a sprinkling of wine vinegar.

NOTE—*Use 2 or 3 additional zucchini if you plan to make Green Pepper Antipasto, p. 148.*

STUFFED TOMATOES

6 *large (beefsteak) tomatoes* (see note)

FILLING

1 *medium onion, finely chopped*
½ *cup bread crumbs*
¼ *cup Parmesan cheese, freshly grated*
½ *cup Swiss cheese, coarsely grated*
2 *tablespoons fresh parsley, finely*
   chopped
¼ *cup pine nuts (optional)*
   salt and freshly ground pepper

} *mixed together*

butter

Preheat the oven to 350° F.

Slice the tops from the tomatoes and scoop the pulp into a strainer. Sprinkle the insides of the tomatoes with salt and invert them to drain.

Drain all the liquid from the tomato pulp by pressing it in the strainer, chop it and add it to the filling. Pack the tomato shells with the filling, dot the tops with butter and bake uncovered on a buttered pan for about 30 minutes. Brown the tops under the broiler for a few minutes if necessary. Serve at room temperature.

NOTE—*If you plan to make Green Pepper Antipasto, p. 148, use 9 tomatoes and increase the filling, using 1 large onion, ¾ cup bread crumbs, ½ cup Parmesan cheese, ¾ cup Swiss cheese and 3 tablespoons parsley.*

BAKED EGGPLANT

Of the many fine ways to prepare eggplant, this may very well be the best.

2 *eggplants, sliced in half lengthwise with stem end*
   removed (see note)

146

> 4 strips uncooked bacon, minced
> 4 cloves garlic, minced
> 1 tablespoon fresh marjoram, chopped,
>   or 1 teaspoon dried marjoram
> 1 teaspoon salt
>   freshly ground pepper

} *mashed together*

½ cup olive oil

Preheat the oven to 350° F.

Using a sharp knife, score the cut surfaces of each eggplant cross-wise, every inch or so, so that the seasonings can penetrate. Divide the bacon mixture into four parts and spread it evenly over the scored eggplant halves. Put them in a baking dish, cut side up, and drizzle the olive oil over them. Cover the pan tightly with foil and bake for about 1 hour.

Put the eggplant on a platter and pour the pan juices over it. Slice and serve at room temperature.

NOTE—*If you plan to make Green Pepper Antipasto, p. 148, you will need some extra eggplant. Cook 3 eggplants, season them with 6 slices of bacon, 6 cloves of garlic, 1½ teaspoons marjoram and 1½ teaspoons salt, and use ¾ cup of olive oil for cooking them.*

CHARCOAL-BROILED PEACHES

A good way to use the coals still glowing when the steak is done—and a wonderful way to eat peaches.

> 6 large peaches, cut in half lengthwise with stones
>   removed
> ¼ cup brandy
> 2 tablespoons brown sugar
>   butter

Place the peach halves, cut side up, on a piece of heavy-duty foil that has been perforated with a fork or skewer every inch or so. Fill the cavity in each peach half with 1 teaspoon of brandy, ½ teaspoon of brown sugar and a piece of butter the size of a peanut. Put the foil on a charcoal grill, quite near the coals, and cook for 10–15 minutes, until the butter and sugar have melted and the peaches are hot.

SUNDAY LUNCH

Green Pepper Antipasto
Cold Tomato Soup Puree
Sliced Steak Sandwiches

·

Amaretti

GREEN PEPPER ANTIPASTO

It's simple to combine Saturday night's vegetables into a most deliciously complicated filling for raw peppers.

> 3 *large green peppers, sliced in half, washed and dried,*
> *with seeds removed*
> *about 2 cups Sautéed Zucchini, p. 148*
> *about 1 Baked Eggplant, p. 146* | *chopped and*
> 2–3 *Stuffed Tomatoes, p. 146* | *mixed together*
> *salt and freshly ground pepper*

Make sure the chopped vegetables are well seasoned and use them to fill the green pepper halves.

Serve at room temperature, sprinkled with fresh chopped parsley, basil or tarragon.

COLD TOMATO SOUP PUREE

Chunky Tomato Soup, p. 142

½ cup light cream

Prepare *Chunky Tomato Soup*. Cool it and put it through a food mill or puree it in an electric blender. Chill well.

Stir in the cream and sprinkle with chopped basil or parsley before serving.

AMARETTI

These Italian macaroons have a distinct almond flavor. Serve them with a full-bodied red wine for a sweet, light dessert.

   1 *pound shelled almonds*
   2 *cups confectioners' sugar*
   2 *tablespoons vanilla*
   ½ *teaspoon almond extract*
   2 *egg whites* (see note)

Preheat the oven to 350° F.

Grind the almonds in an electric blender until they are very fine. Put them in a small bowl, add the sugar, the vanilla and the almond extract and work everything together with your fingers until it is well blended. Stir in the unbeaten egg whites. The dough will be quite sticky. Drop it by the teaspoonful onto buttered cookies sheets and bake the cookies until they are lightly browned, about 15 or 20 minutes.

This recipe will make about 48 *Amaretti*, more than you should need. We hear they keep for weeks, but we've never had a chance to find out.

NOTE—*Reserved when making* Spaghetti alla Carbonara, *p. 140, we hope.*

Menus for
OCTOBER

FRIDAY DINNER

Sausage and Peppers
Hero Rolls

•

Pears and Grapes

SATURDAY LUNCH

Cottage Cheese Pancakes
Sour Cream and Chives
Sliced Tomatoes

·

Applesauce
Nut Cookies

SATURDAY DINNER

Roast Beef
Sautéed Peppers and Onions
Baked Butternut Squash

·

Frozen Syllabub

SUNDAY LUNCH

Pasta al Pesto
Green Salad

·

Pears Savoie

Preparation Schedule

for

OCTOBER

[ALL RECIPES SERVE 6]

These are menus for a lazy autumn weekend—you'll have lots of time to rake leaves and enjoy the fall colors. It's a casual weekend, with no split-second timing; everything except the pasta can wait awhile or be reheated before serving. The fruits and vegetables in these recipes are at their prime in October, but you may choose to use this weekend's menus at other times of the year, too, since the meals require very little cooking or advance preparation.

In Advance—You can bake the *Nut Cookies* in advance, but because they are among the few elegant confections that are truly easy to make, we sometimes save their preparation as a special weekend treat for young children who are often excluded from really interesting kitchen jobs. If you are using fresh basil for the pesto sauce on Sunday, you should prepare the *Basil Puree* a few days ahead. If the puree comes from your freezer, you have only to defrost it on Sunday morning.

On Friday—The *Sausage and Peppers* for Friday night's dinner is a simple, one-skillet meal that can be prepared several hours ahead or just before serving and will also provide the *Sautéed Peppers and Onions* for Saturday's dinner.

On Saturday—On Saturday morning, make the *Applesauce*, the *Syllabub* and mix the batter for the *Cottage Cheese Pancakes*.

While you are cooking the *Roast Beef* for Saturday's dinner, bake the *Butternut Squash* in the same oven until it is soft. When the roast is done, take it out of the oven and let it rest awhile before you carve it—time enough to put the finishing touches on the squash and reheat it.

On Sunday—You can cook the *Pears Savoie* any time Sunday morning and put them in the oven 15 minutes before you serve lunch. Since you will already have prepared the basil puree, you can make the *Pasta al Pesto* in the time it takes to cook the linguine.

FRIDAY DINNER

Sausage and Peppers
Hero Rolls

.

Pears and Grapes

SAUSAGE AND PEPPERS

2 *large Bermuda onions, sliced* (see note)
4 *large green peppers, seeded and sliced* (see note)
  olive oil
  salt and freshly ground pepper

3 *pounds Italian sausage, sweet, hot or mixed*

Heat enough olive oil to cover the bottom of a large, heavy skillet or dutch oven. Separate the onions into rings and sauté them, stirring frequently, until they are transparent but not brown. Add the peppers and toss them with the onions over high heat until the peppers are slightly cooked but still crisp and bright green. Season to taste with salt and freshly ground black pepper and remove them from the pan. [Set aside enough to serve on Saturday night.]

Brown the sausages in the pan, cover and continue to cook until the sausages are done. Pour off the fat and brown the sausages a little more. Just before serving, add the cooked onions and peppers and stir, scraping the brown bits from the bottom of the pan into the mixture. Cook just until the vegetables are heated through.

If you are not cooking extra peppers and onions, you may begin this dish by cooking the sausages, pouring off the extra fat, and then adding the uncooked onions and peppers to the pan. Sauté them with the sausages until they are tender.

NOTE—*If you plan to serve* Sautéed Peppers and Onions *on Saturday, double the number of peppers and onions and set aside half the vegetables. Serve them on Saturday at room temperature.*

SATURDAY LUNCH

Cottage Cheese Pancakes
Sour Cream and Chives
Sliced Tomatoes

·

Applesauce
Nut Cookies

COTTAGE CHEESE PANCAKES

Serve these pancakes with chilled white wine for an unexpected touch of elegance.

4 eggs, separated
1 cup cottage cheese
1 cup sour cream
1 cup flour
2 tablespoons chives, chopped
salt and freshly ground pepper

sour cream
chopped chives

Beat the egg whites until they are stiff but not dry.

In another bowl, combine the cottage cheese, sour cream and egg yolks and beat in the flour, the chives and some salt and pepper. Fold the beaten egg whites into the batter.

Drop the batter by the tablespoon onto a well-buttered griddle and cook the pancakes over moderate heat until they are slightly crisp on both sides. Keep them warm on a platter in a very low oven until all the batter has been used.

Serve with sour cream and chopped chives.

APPLESAUCE

It is always a good idea to make large quantities of applesauce since it freezes well and is a pleasant thing to have on hand throughout the year. Although apples are always available, the time to make lots of applesauce is, of course, in the fall when they are fresh, plentiful and cheap. McIntosh and tart green apples make the best sauce.

4 pounds apples (12–15 apples)
  brown sugar

Cut the apples into chunks. Put them in a large pot and add enough water or apple juice to just cover the bottom of the pot. Cook, covered, over low heat, stirring frequently and adding more liquid if necessary to prevent the apples from sticking and burning. When the apples are soft, remove them from the heat, put them through a food mill or sieve and discard the skin and core. Add brown sugar to taste.

Four pounds of apples will produce about 6 cups of sauce.

NUT COOKIES

1 cup sweet butter, softened
5 tablespoons confectioners' sugar
1½ teaspoons vanilla
2 cups flour
¼ teaspoon salt
1½ cups finely chopped nuts (pecans or walnuts)

  confectioners' sugar

Preheat the oven to 325° F.

Cream the butter and sugar together with a wooden spoon. Add the vanilla, flour, salt and nuts and use your fingers to blend them into what will be a very crumbly dough. Form the dough into crescent-shaped cookies with your fingers.

Bake on an ungreased cookie sheet until the cookies are lightly browned, about 20 minutes. Roll them in confectioners' sugar while they are still hot. You will have about 36 cookies.

SATURDAY DINNER

Roast Beef
Sautéed Peppers and Onions
Baked Butternut Squash

·

Frozen Syllabub

ROAST BEEF

If you are cooking a rib roast, 3 ribs will serve 6 people. A rolled roast—preferably cross-rib or sirloin—is cheaper and goes further; 3 pounds should be enough. A good piece of meat needs no seasoning.

Allow the meat to come to room temperature, and preheat the oven to 325° F. Roast, uncovered, allowing about 20 minutes a pound for medium rare, 25 minutes a pound if the roast is boneless. Use a meat thermometer as well—it's the best way to be sure that the meat is done as you like it.

SAUTÉED PEPPERS AND ONIONS

If you served Sausage and Peppers on Friday night, you will have these all ready.

2 *large Bermuda onions, sliced*
4 *large green peppers, seeded and sliced*
   olive oil
   salt and freshly ground pepper

158

Heat enough olive oil to cover the bottom of a large, heavy skillet or dutch oven. Separate the onions into rings and sauté them, stirring frequently, until they are transparent but not brown. Add the peppers and toss them with the onions over high heat until the peppers are slightly cooked but still crisp and bright green. Season to taste with salt and freshly ground black pepper and remove them from the pan. Serve at room temperature.

BAKED BUTTERNUT SQUASH

1 large or 2 small butternut squash (about 4 pounds)
* butter*
* salt and freshly ground pepper*

Preheat the oven to 325° F.

Place the whole squash in a baking pan, add ½ cup of water, cover tightly with foil and bake it until it is tender when pierced with the point of a sharp knife—about 1–1½ hours. Cut the squash in half and scoop out the seeds. Peel the squash and mash it with plenty of butter, salt and pepper to taste.

FROZEN SYLLABUB

Syllabub, a frothy whip of wine, sugar and cream, is an old English dessert, an ancient ancestor of the trifle.

1 cup heavy cream
1 cup confectioners' sugar
½ cup dry white wine or sherry
* juice and grated rind of 1 lemon*

Beat the cream until it begins to thicken. Gradually beat in the sugar and then the wine, lemon juice and rind. Put the bowl in the freezer, but try not to let it touch the floor or sides—this will prevent the syllabub from crystallizing as it freezes. It will take about 3 hours to freeze solid, but it's also good before it has completely frozen.

SUNDAY LUNCH

Pasta al Pesto
Green Salad

·

Pears Savoie

PASTA AL PESTO

Magnifica!

The basis of pesto sauce is a highly concentrated fresh basil puree. Those of us who grow basil in our own gardens know that it is just as easy to grow a lot of basil as a little and well worth it, since the basic pesto puree can be used in many ways other than as a pasta sauce. A teaspoon or two makes a delicious seasoning for soups, rice, potatoes, fish or meat.

We are pesto fanatics and always have a generous supply of basil puree stored away in our freezers by the end of summer. You can freeze enough pesto for a pound of pasta in a plastic or paper cup and quickly defrost it when you wish. There is nothing more delightfully unexpected than the smell of fresh basil on a cold January day.

The basil leaves for pesto are traditionally pureed with a mortar and pestle (hence its name). We find it just as satisfactory to use a blender—and infinitely easier. In all other respects, however, we are unbending purists, for we believe that this superb sauce deserves to be made with generous quantities of the best ingredients you can get. Not only should the Parmesan cheese be freshly grated, but it should be of high quality. So should the olive oil. Above all, do not attempt to make pesto unless you have *fresh* basil (an excellent alternative pasta sauce is given for those who do not).

> 2–4 *cups basil leaves, including flowers and tender stems*
>   *about ½ cup olive oil*
> ¾ *cup Parmesan cheese, freshly grated*
>   2 *cloves garlic, minced*
> ¼ *cup pine nuts (optional)*
>   *lots of salt and freshly ground pepper*
> 1½ *pounds linguine or fettucine*
> ¼ *cup butter, softened*
>
>   *more freshly grated Parmesan cheese*

Pesto is an uncooked sauce.

Put most of the olive oil in a blender container. Gradually blend in the basil until you have a thick, smooth puree. To make the blending easier, use a thick basil stem to push the leaves down into the oil as the puree thickens. Cautiously add more oil, only if you need it to puree the basil. [If you are making pesto for future use, it is now ready to be frozen.]

Put the puree in a bowl. Add the cheese, garlic, pine nuts, about 1 teaspoon of salt and some pepper, and stir thoroughly.

Cook the pasta in boiling, salted water until it is just tender. While it is cooking, add about ¼ of a cup of the boiling water to the pesto. Drain the pasta and rinse it quickly with very hot water. Put the pasta back in the pot and toss it with the butter over very low heat until the butter has melted. Add the sauce and toss very well to distribute it evenly throughout the pasta.

Serve immediately, and pass around a bowl of grated cheese, salt and a pepper mill.

SPAGHETTINI WITH ANCHOVY SAUCE

This is our alternative to Pasta al Pesto. It is embarrassingly easy to make and hardly seems serious—until you taste it, that is.

3   *two-ounce cans anchovy fillets, chopped*
    olive oil
4–5 *cloves garlic, minced*
1½ *pounds spaghettini*
    freshly ground pepper
½   *cup chopped parsley*

Combine the oil from the anchovy cans with enough additional oil to make ¾ of a cup. Heat this oil in a small skillet, add the garlic and cook it for a minute or two. Add the anchovies and cook, stirring gently. They will dissolve into the sauce.

Cook the pasta in boiling, salted water until it is just done. While it is cooking, add ¼ cup of the cooking water to the anchovy sauce. Add the pepper and parsley.

Drain the pasta and rinse quickly with very hot water. Stir the sauce briefly, pour it over the hot pasta and toss well. Serve immediately.

GREEN SALAD

A mixed salad including arugola, called rocket in some areas, would be perfect with this meal. If you can't find any arugola, include some watercress among the greens in this salad, and choose a variety of lettuces—whatever is freshest when you go to the market.

Wash the greens, shake out the water and dry them by rolling them in a terry towel. Break the greens into bite-sized pieces. Toss them in the dressing before serving.

VINAIGRETTE DRESSING

1½ *tablespoons wine vinegar*
4 *tablespoons olive oil* ⎫ *beaten together well*
1 *small clove garlic, minced* ⎬ *with a fork*
  salt and freshly ground pepper ⎭

PEARS SAVOIE

6–8 *pears, peeled, cored and sliced in thin wedges*
  butter
2 *tablespoons sugar*
  1-inch piece of vanilla bean (or 1 teaspoon vanilla
    mixed with the cream)
½ *cup heavy cream*

Preheat the oven to 325° F.

Using a pan that can go from burner to oven to table, melt some butter over moderate heat and arrange the pears in the pan, in one layer if possible. Sprinkle the sugar over the pears and add the vanilla bean. Cook the pears gently until they are soft, 10–30 minutes depending on the ripeness of the pears. Add the cream and cook for 2 or 3 minutes, then place the pears in the oven for 15 minutes.

Serve them hot or warm. They may be left in the warm oven, with the heat turned off, while dinner is being served.

Menus for
NOVEMBER

FRIDAY DINNER

Sweet and Sour Meatballs
Buttered Noodles
Sautéed Escarole

·

Turnovers

SATURDAY LUNCH

Sausage Yorkshire Pudding
Cole Slaw

·

Sliced Grapefruit and Oranges

SATURDAY DINNER

Blanquette de Veau
Rice
Steamed Broccoli

·

Granita al Caffè

SUNDAY LUNCH

Meatball Hero Sandwiches
Caraway Cole Slaw

·

Apples and Pears

Preparation Schedule

for

NOVEMBER

[ALL RECIPES SERVE 6]

Most of this weekend's cooking can be done either in advance or during the weekend—it's entirely a matter of your own preference.

In Advance—Only one dish—the *Sweet and Sour Meatballs*—really should be made in advance, since it will taste better after mellowing in the refrigerator for a few days. The *Turnovers* can be made a day ahead, or weeks in advance if you freeze them. Don't make the *Cole Slaw* for Saturday more than one day ahead since you will serve it a second time on Sunday. We tell you in the recipe how to prepare the *Blanquette de Veau* entirely in advance, if you wish, but we would probably compromise, cooking the meat ahead of time and leaving the vegetables and the sauce until an hour before Saturday's dinner. Make the *Granita* whenever you'll be around to stir it from time to time. It will keep for several days in the freezer but must be made at least four hours in advance.

On Friday—Cook the *Noodles* and sauté the *Escarole* on Friday night while you are reheating the meatballs.

On Saturday—On Saturday, slice the *Grapefruit and Oranges* while the *Sausage Yorkshire Pudding* is baking, and serve everything together for a one-course brunch. At dinner time cook the *Rice* and the *Broccoli* while you're assembling the *Blanquette*.

FRIDAY DINNER

Sweet and Sour Meatballs
Buttered Noodles
Sautéed Escarole

·

Turnovers

SWEET AND SOUR MEATBALLS

SAUCE
  4 *tablespoons butter*
  2 *large onions, coarsely diced*
  2 *tablespoons flour*
  4 *cups beef broth*
  ¾ *cup currants (or raisins)*
    juice and coarsely grated rind of 1 lemon
  ⅓ *cup vinegar*
  ½ *cup brown sugar*
  1 *dozen ginger snaps, crumbled (or 1 teaspoon powdered*
      ginger and 2 tablespoons flour)
    salt to taste

MEATBALLS (see note)
  3 *pounds chopped beef*
  1 *medium onion, finely chopped*
  ½ *cup bread crumbs*
  2 *teaspoons salt*
    freshly ground pepper
    several generous dashes of Worcestershire and Tabasco
      Sauce
  2 *eggs*

Preheat the oven to 400° F.

To make the sauce, melt the butter in a large pot, add the onions and sauté them briefly. Blend in the flour over low heat, gradually stir in the beef broth and continue cooking over moderate heat, stirring frequently, until the sauce thickens slightly. Add the currants, lemon rind and juice, vinegar, brown sugar, ginger snaps and salt and simmer, stirring from time to time, while you are preparing the meatballs.

Combine the meatball ingredients thoroughly in a large bowl and form the mixture into small meatballs about the size of walnuts. Put the meatballs on cookie sheets (or heavy-duty aluminum foil) and brown them in the oven for about 15 minutes, until they are cooked through.

Taste the sauce and adjust the seasonings, adding more vinegar or sugar, if necessary, to achieve the proper balance between sweet and sour. Add the meatballs to the sauce and cook them over low heat for 15–20 minutes more.

These meatballs may be kept in the refrigerator for several days; their flavor will only improve. They may also be frozen.

NOTE—Sweet and Sour Meatballs *make a wonderful filling for the* Hero Sandwiches *on the menu for Sunday's lunch, p. 176. If you're planning to serve the sandwiches, you'll need more meatballs, of course—just add another pound of meat, an extra onion and one more teaspoon of salt to the meatball mixture. There will still be plenty of sauce.*

BUTTERED NOODLES

Cook ¾ of a pound of broad noodles according to the directions on the package, drain them and toss them with salt and a little butter, just enough to keep them from sticking together.

SAUTÉED ESCAROLE

Cooked escarole has a slightly bitter taste. Some people love it, some don't. If you don't, make an escarole salad, following the recipe for *Chicory Salad*, p. 37.

1 *large head escarole, washed and cut up as for salad*
  olive oil
  salt
  juice of 1 lemon (2–3 tablespoons)

Heat a little olive oil in a large pot, add the escarole, sprinkle it with some salt and the lemon juice and toss it over fairly high heat until it is wilted. Serve it hot.

TURNOVERS

These tiny, rich pastries are a bit of a bother to make but well worth it.

PASTRY
½ *cup (4 ounces) cream cheese, at room temperature*
½ *cup butter, at room temperature*
 1 *cup flour*

SUGGESTED FILLINGS
  apricot, raspberry or plum jam
3 *apples, peeled, thinly sliced and sautéed in a little butter until barely tender*

To make the dough, combine the cream cheese, butter and flour lightly with your fingers. Form the mixture into a ball and let it chill for about an hour.

Preheat the oven to 350° F.

Roll out the dough on a well-floured board until it is reasonably thin (about ⅛ inch). Cut it into circles with the rim of a glass about

3 inches in diameter. Place a scant teaspoon of filling to one side of the center of each pastry circle. Using a spatula if necessary, fold the pastry in half and press the edges down well with a fork to form semi-circular turnovers.

Place the turnovers on ungreased cookie sheets or heavy aluminum foil and bake them until they are lightly browned, about 20–30 minutes. Remove them from the pan with a spatula while they are still hot.

This recipe will make about 24 pastries.

SATURDAY LUNCH

Sausage Yorkshire Pudding
Cole Slaw

·

Sliced Grapefruit and
Oranges

SAUSAGE YORKSHIRE PUDDING

1½ *pounds small link breakfast sausages*
 1 *cup flour*
 ½ *teaspoon salt*
 1 *cup milk*
 2 *eggs*
 1 *tablespoon chives, chopped (or 1 finely chopped scal-*
      lion, including green part)

Preheat the oven to 450° F.

Fry the sausages in an oven-proof skillet, or broil them in a shallow baking pan about 9 by 13 inches. When they are crisp and brown, drain off most of the fat, leaving just enough to cover the bottom of the pan.

While the sausages are cooking, combine the flour and the salt in a large bowl, and add the milk gradually, beating until the mixture is smooth. Beat the eggs in a separate bowl for about two minutes, and add them and the chives to the flour mixture, beating it all very well. (This batter can be made in an electric blender.)

Making certain that the fat in the bottom of the pan is very hot, pour the batter over the sausages. Bake for 15 minutes at 450°, turn the oven down to 350°, and continue to bake for about 10 minutes more until the pudding has puffed up and turned golden brown. Serve it immediately.

COLE SLAW

If you want to have enough Cole Slaw to serve again on Sunday, double this recipe. Try combining red and white cabbages—it looks very pretty. To change the Cole Slaw a bit before serving it the second time, stir in a tablespoon or two of caraway seeds.

1 head (about 2 pounds) red or white cabbage, shredded
1 small onion, grated

DRESSING
½ cup mayonnaise
½ cup sour cream
juice of 1 lemon (2–3 tablespoons) ⎱ *mixed together*
sugar to taste
salt and freshly ground pepper

Combine the cabbage and onion and toss them in the dressing. Refrigerate until ready to serve.

SLICED GRAPEFRUIT AND ORANGES

2 grapefruits
4 oranges
1 small can Bing cherries (optional)

Slice each grapefruit and orange in half vertically, cutting through the stem ends. Place each half with the cut side down and slice it into very thin semicircles. Arrange the slices on a platter and decorate them with cherries, if you wish.

There's no need to serve plates or spoons with this. Just put a small plate on the table for the discarded rinds.

SATURDAY DINNER

Blanquette de Veau
Rice
Steamed Broccoli

·

Granita al Caffè

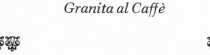

BLANQUETTE DE VEAU

This is a delicate dish in which simple elements combine to make a rich, distinctive sauce. We prefer scallions to the traditional onions both for their flavor and their fresh color.

3 pounds boneless veal shoulder, cut into 1½-inch cubes
4 cups chicken broth

1 *onion stuck with 1 clove*
½ *teaspoon thyme*
1 *bay leaf*
4 *peppercorns*

butter
3 *bunches scallions, cleaned and trimmed to 6-inch lengths*
½ *pound small whole mushrooms*
salt and freshly ground pepper

SAUCE
4 *tablespoons butter*
4 *tablespoons flour*
3 *cups stock (from the veal)*
2 *egg yolks*
½ *cup heavy cream* } *beaten together with a fork*
½ *lemon*
salt and freshly ground pepper

Put the veal in a large pot, pour the broth over it, slowly bring it to a boil and simmer it for 5–10 minutes, skimming off any scum from the surface. Add the onion, thyme, bay leaf and peppercorns, cover the pot and simmer the veal gently for 1–1½ hours until it is tender but not falling apart.

While the meat is cooking, prepare the vegetables. Melt some butter in a frying pan and sauté the scallions, seasoning them with salt and pepper, until they are just tender and bright green. Remove the scallions and sauté the mushrooms in the pan for about 5 minutes, adding salt, pepper and more butter if necessary.

When the veal is done put it on a large platter, arrange the vegetables around it and keep it all warm in a low oven. Strain the stock.

To make the sauce, melt the butter in a saucepan, blend in the flour and cook gently for a minute or two. Gradually add the veal stock, stirring constantly until the sauce is smooth. Simmer the sauce for 10–15 minutes, stirring frequently. Keeping the heat as low as possible, add the cream and egg yolk mixture and stir constantly for another 2 or 3 minutes. Do not allow the sauce to boil after adding the egg yolks or it will curdle. Season it carefully with lemon juice, salt and pepper.

Pour the sauce over the meat and vegetables. Serve with rice.

Except for adding the cream and egg yolks, the *blanquette* can be prepared a day or two in advance, but it should not be assembled until you are ready to serve it. After the meat and vegetables are cooked, put them in a container with ½ cup of the strained stock. Make the sauce with the remaining stock and store it separately. To assemble, place the meat and stock in a pot, lay the vegetables on top of the meat and heat very gently. Put them on a platter and keep it warm. Add the hot stock to the sauce, heat it and add the egg yolks and cream, proceeding as above.

STEAMED BROCCOLI

Wash a large bunch of broccoli. Peel the stems with a potato peeler and cut the broccoli into serving pieces.

Bring about 2 inches of lightly salted water to a rapid boil in a large pot. Put the broccoli stem end down in the boiling water and cover the pot tightly. Cook it fast. Cooking time for broccoli will vary depending on its size and freshness, but it usually takes 10–15 minutes. Pierce a stem with the point of a sharp knife to see if it is tender. The broccoli will turn bright green and should still be that color when it is done—don't overcook it. Drain it well before serving.

Leftover broccoli is delicious cold with a simple dressing of oil and lemon juice.

GRANITA AL CAFFÈ

A *granita* is an Italian water ice, a light and satisfying dessert after a rich meal. It can be made in many lovely flavors. We especially like this espresso ice—dessert and coffee at the same time.

> *3 cups boiling water*
> *6 heaping tablespoons espresso coffee*
> *3 tablespoons sugar*

*½ cup heavy cream, whipped, or ½ cup double cream,
p. 97.*

Following your usual method, brew extra strong coffee using the proportions given above. Stir in the sugar and put the coffee in the refrigerator to cool. When it is cool, pour the coffee into a metal bowl and put it in the freezer.

After an hour or so, when the *granita* begins to solidify, stir it and break up the frozen portions into fine crystals. Try to do this about every half hour, using a fork or a potato masher, until the *granita* has completely crystallized. Freezing time, depending on your freezer, will be from 3 to 4 hours. Once it has crystallized, *granita* will keep for several days in the freezer without solidifying.

Serve the *granita* in individual bowls with a dab of whipped cream, double cream or chocolate or vanilla ice cream on each portion.

SUNDAY LUNCH

*Meatball Hero Sandwiches
Caraway Cole Slaw*

.

Apples and Pears

MEATBALL HERO SANDWICHES

Sweet and Sour Meatballs, p. 168.

1 *large Italian bread, or 6 individual hero rolls*
  butter (optional)
  sliced tomatoes (optional)

You may, of course, use individual hero rolls for these sandwiches, but we prefer to use a large Italian bread. Slice the bread in half lengthwise, fill it and then slice it diagonally into 6 sandwiches.

The meatball filling is equally delicious hot or cold. If you decide to use it hot, reheat the meatballs in their sauce and use plenty of sauce in the sandwiches. If you use a cold meatball filling, you may wish to butter the bread and add some sliced tomatoes, so that the sandwiches will not be dry.

Menus for
DECEMBER

FRIDAY DINNER

Smoked Mixed Grill
Spoon Bread
Zucchini Salad

•

Hot Bananas

SATURDAY LUNCH

Sweet Pea Soup
Cheese Sticks
Spanish Onion Sandwiches
·

Grandma Mae's Cookies
Ice Cream

SATURDAY DINNER

Choucroute Garni
Boiled Potatoes
Pumpernickel
·

Apple Crisp Tart

SUNDAY LUNCH

Omelette Provençale
Green Salad
French Bread
·

Prunes Crème Fraîche

Preparation Schedule

for

DECEMBER

[ALL RECIPES SERVE 6]

In Advance—*Crème Fraîche*, used in Friday's and Sunday's desserts, is the only thing you *must* prepare well in advance for this weekend, but we strongly suggest that you make the *Choucroute Garni* and the *Zucchini Salad* a day or so ahead and bake *Grandma Mae's Cookies* before the weekend begins. You can make the *Sweet Pea Soup* for Saturday's lunch any time from Friday morning on, but don't add the cream and butter until you reheat the soup just before serving.

On Friday—While the *Spoon Bread* is baking on Friday night, cook the meats for the *Smoked Mixed Grill* and fix the sauce and nuts for the *Hot Bananas*. If you prefer, cook the smoked meats about an hour or so ahead and slowly reheat them before serving.

On Saturday—Bake the *Apple Crisp Tart* and the *Cheese Sticks* before lunch on Saturday. Prepare the *Spanish Onion Sandwiches* for lunch while the soup is heating.

About an hour before dinner, add any meat left from Friday's mixed grill to the *Choucroute*, reheat it in the oven and boil the *Potatoes*.

On Sunday—On Sunday, fix the *Prunes Crème Fraîche* first, then make the salad while the vegetables for the *Omelette Provençale* are cooking.

181

FRIDAY DINNER

Smoked Mixed Grill
Spoon Bread
Zucchini Salad

·

Hot Bananas

SMOKED MIXED GRILL

Everything for this dish can be "grilled" in the same frying pan and you don't even have to do it at the last minute. Pick one from Group A, two from Group B for a nice assortment.

½ pound bacon, thickly sliced

Group A
  smoked pork chops
  ham steak, cut into individual portions
  slices of smoked pork butt or shoulder

Group B
  Canadian bacon
  fresh pork sausage patties or link breakfast sausage
  smoked sausage
  knackwurst

½ pound mushrooms
½ box of cherry tomatoes

Fry the bacon in a large skillet. When it is crisp, remove it from the pan and pour off the fat. Put the fresh sausages in the pan, cook them thoroughly, pour off most of the fat and brown the other meats in the same pan. Add the mushrooms during the last 4 or 5 minutes of browning and put in the cherry tomatoes just before you turn off the heat. They should heat through without cooking.

You can cook this dish about an hour in advance and reheat it slowly before serving.

If you have not prepared Saturday's *Choucroute Garni*, p. 189, in advance, you can cook the meat for the *Smoked Mixed Grill* and for the *Choucroute* at the same time. Set aside about 3 pounds of assorted meats to add later to the *Choucroute*.

Any meat left from the *Smoked Mixed Grill* will be a pleasant addition to the *Choucroute*, even if you *have* made it in advance. Just bury the leftover meat in the *Choucroute* before reheating.

SPOON BREAD

This Southern classic has the lightness of a soufflé and the down-to-earth flavor of cornbread.

 4 *tablespoons butter*
2½ *cups milk*
 1 *cup cornmeal*
 1 *teaspoon salt*
 4 *eggs, separated*

Preheat the oven to 375° F.

Put the butter in a 2-quart baking dish and let it melt in the oven. Bring 2 cups of the milk to a boil in a large saucepan and whisk in the cornmeal and salt. Remove the pan from the heat and continue to beat for a minute or two until the mixture is thick and smooth. Blend in the melted butter and ½ cup of cold milk and beat in the egg yolks. Beat the egg whites until they are stiff but not dry and fold them into the batter.

Pour the batter into the hot baking dish and bake the spoon bread until it is puffed and brown, about 30 minutes.

Spoon it from the baking dish and pass around lots of butter.

Spoon bread makes a marvelous breakfast. Serve it with bacon and jam, or fold about a cup of diced cooked ham or sausage into the batter after beating in the egg yolks. Some people prefer spoon bread slightly sweetened; if you want to try it that way, add 2 teaspoons of sugar when you add the salt.

ZUCCHINI SALAD

Olive oil
2 *large cloves garlic, minced*
6 *medium zucchini, coarsely diced* (see note)
1 *teaspoon salt*
  freshly ground pepper
3 *tablespoons tomato paste*
2 *large green peppers, diced*

Heat enough oil to cover the bottom of a large skillet, add the minced garlic and cook it for a minute or two. Add the zucchini, salt, pepper and tomato paste to the pan and cook over medium heat, stirring constantly, for about five minutes or so. The zucchini should still be very crisp.

Remove the pan from the heat and stir in the green pepper. Serve at room temperature.

NOTE—*Cook 2 more zucchini and increase the other ingredients accordingly if you plan to make* Omelette Provençale, *p. 192.*

HOT BANANAS

Cooked bananas are delicious; unfortunately, they are often turned into an unpalatable mush by overcooking. We like them warm and well sauced, but still firm.

½ *cup rum*
3 *tablespoons brown sugar*
  butter
6 *firm bananas, peeled and sliced*

½ cup salted peanuts, coarsely chopped
½ cup crème fraîche, *p. 193* (or ½ cup sour cream
    thinned with a little milk or cream)

Heat the rum in a saucepan, gently so it doesn't catch fire, dissolve the sugar in it and simmer it for a few minutes.

Melt some butter in a skillet, add the bananas and toss them lightly. Pour the rum sauce over them and cook them quickly over a brisk heat, basting them with the sauce, until the bananas are barely heated through but have not changed color or become soft. Sprinkle them with the nuts and serve them immediately with a dollop of *crème fraîche* on each portion.

SATURDAY LUNCH

Sweet Pea Soup
Cheese Sticks
Spanish Onion Sandwiches

•

Grandma Mae's Cookies
Ice Cream

SWEET PEA SOUP

  3 cups homemade chicken stock (or canned broth, if
    necessary)
  1 large onion, thinly sliced
  1 small carrot, thinly sliced
3–4 lettuce leaves
  2 pounds fresh peas, shelled, or 2 ten-ounce packages
    frozen baby peas (not in butter sauce)

½–1 cup cream or milk
¼ cup sweet butter
1 teaspoon sugar
salt and freshly ground pepper

Bring the broth to a boil, add the onion, carrot and lettuce, cover and cook over medium heat for about 10 minutes. Add the peas, cover and continue to cook about 15 minutes more or until the peas are just tender. Puree the soup in a blender or put it through a food mill or sieve. Put it back in the pot.

Add the cream, butter and seasonings to the soup and heat it gently until the butter has melted. Serve with Cheese Sticks (see below) or with Croutons, p. 143.

CHEESE STICKS

It doesn't seem to matter how many of these you make. They are like the proverbial peanuts—you will stop eating them only when there are no more left.

1–1¼ cups flour
½ cup cold butter, cut into small pieces
1 egg
8–10 tablespoons Parmesan cheese, freshly grated
½ teaspoon salt

Preheat the oven to 375° F.

Using your fingers, work the butter into 1 cup of the flour until the mixture has the consistency of coarse meal. Break the egg into the mixture and work it all together, forming it into a ball. Add more flour if the dough seems too sticky to handle with ease, then work in the Parmesan cheese and the salt, until they are well incorporated.

Roll small pieces of the dough between your palms to form little sticks about 2 inches long and bake them on ungreased cookie sheets for about 15 minutes or until the sticks are crisp and golden brown.

This is an ideal way to use leftover pie crust dough.

SPANISH ONION SANDWICHES

The fearless will eat an onion and butter sandwich without further embellishment, but most people will probably use a little of everything.

> *pumpernickel bread*
> *unsalted butter*
> *1 large Spanish onion, peeled and thickly sliced*
> *1 large green pepper, seeded and sliced (optional)*
> *6 slices Swiss cheese (optional)*

Arrange all the ingredients on a platter and let people help themselves.

GRANDMA MAE'S COOKIES

We once tried to figure out how many thousands of these cookies she had baked. She always had a supply on hand, neatly packed in coffee tins in the freezer, ready to bring out if we dropped in unexpectedly or a neighbor's child came by for a minute. She never came to visit without bringing along a batch or two, leaving them without ceremony, like a calling card. When the children spent a few days with her, they helped her make them, using an endless variety of shapes and flavorings.

Everyone who knew her has this recipe, but although the cookies always turn out wonderfully well, they are never quite like hers. Some suspect there was a secret ingredient. We think we know what it was. . . .

> *½ cup butter, softened*
> *½ cup vegetable shortening*
> *1 cup dark brown sugar*

1 egg
1 teaspoon vanilla
2 cups flour
½ teaspoon baking powder ⎫ *mixed together*
   pinch of salt ⎭

Cream the butter and the shortening with the brown sugar. Gradually beat in the egg, the vanilla and the dry ingredients and mix thoroughly. Form the dough into two cylinders about 1½ inches in diameter, wrap them in foil and refrigerate for a few hours, overnight if possible.

Preheat the oven to 350° F.

Cut the dough into ¼-inch slices, put the cookies on buttered cookie sheets, make a finger depression in the center of each cookie and fill it with apricot, strawberry or mint jelly. Bake the cookies until they are golden brown, about 10–12 minutes. You will have about 72 cookies.

These cookies freeze well and can be served directly from the freezer without thawing.

SATURDAY DINNER

Choucroute Garni
Boiled Potatoes
Pumpernickel

·

Apple Crisp Tart

CHOUCROUTE GARNI

Choucroute Garni is especially good to prepare for a large crowd, since it is not much more trouble to make a lot than a little and, with a judicious choice of meats, it can be quite reasonable in cost.

Don't worry about where to find the ingredients you need. Most supermarkets stock an interesting assortment of sausages these days, and you can try them out—the greater the variety, the better. Look for juniper berries in the spice department; if you can't get them, stir in ¼ cup of gin 15 minutes before the Choucroute is done. As for the sauerkraut, try to find a delicatessen that sells it in bulk; it is the best by far. If you cannot buy it "fresh," look for it in jars or packages—both are superior to canned sauerkraut, which may also be used but should be soaked first in several changes of water for at least an hour.

Choucroute Garni keeps well and can be frozen.

    6 slices bacon, cut into small pieces
    2 large onions, chopped
    2 carrots, thinly sliced
    4 pounds sauerkraut, preferably fresh, washed in cold
          water and squeezed dry
    2 cups dry white wine
    2 cups chicken broth
       a bouquet garni:
          6 sprigs parsley
          2 bay leaves   tied together in a
          8 peppercorns, bruised   piece of cheesecloth
          8 juniper berries, bruised
       butter
2–3 pounds assorted meats, cut into small serving pieces:
          smoked pork chops; assorted sausages, both bland
          and hot (knackwurst, kielbassa, fresh pork sausage,
          etc.); leftover ham or pork. Leftover pieces of roast
          duck or goose are a particularly pleasing addition.
          As a matter of fact, if you are making this for a
          large group, it seems well worth roasting a small
          bird for this dish alone.

3 pounds new potatoes, boiled in their skins (see note)

Preheat the oven to 325° F.

Cook the bacon briefly in a heavy casserole, add one chopped onion and the carrots and cook them in the bacon drippings until the onion wilts. Add the sauerkraut, mix it well into the vegetables, add the wine and stock and bury the bouquet garni in the mixture. Cover the casserole, bring it to a boil and place it in the oven for 1 hour.

While the sauerkraut is cooking, brown the remaining onion in a little butter, add the meats and brown them well. After the sauerkraut has cooked for an hour, take it out of the oven and bury the meats and the pan juices in the sauerkraut. Return the covered casserole to the oven for another hour of braising. Before serving, remove the bouquet garni and season with salt if necessary.

Serve with boiled potatoes and/or pumpernickel. Choucroute Garni can be made entirely in advance and reheated on top of the stove or in the oven.

NOTE—*Make 3 or 4 extra potatoes for the Omelette Provençale, p. 192.*

APPLE CRISP TART

CRUST (see note)
1–1¼ cups flour
dash of salt
½ cup cold butter, cut into small pieces
1 egg

FILLING
6–8 medium apples, about 2½ pounds, preferably Mc-Intosh

TOPPING
¾ cup brown sugar
6 tablespoons flour
¼ cup cold butter, cut into small pieces
1 teaspoon cinnamon (optional)
¼ cup walnuts, coarsely chopped (optional)

Put a cup of flour and the salt in a mixing bowl and work in the butter with your fingers until the mixture has the consistency of meal. Add the egg, work it into the mixture and form the dough into a ball, adding a little more flour if the dough is too sticky to handle easily. Using your fingers, press a little more than half of the dough into a pie plate, or a 9- or 10-inch springform pan or flan ring, forming sides about 1 inch high. Refrigerate. [Set aside the remaining dough to make Cheese Sticks, p. 186.]

Preheat the oven to 375° F.

Peel, core and slice the apples and blend the topping ingredients together lightly with a fork or your fingers. Put the apples in the pie shell and sprinkle the topping evenly over them.

Bake the tart on the lowest shelf of the oven for about 45 minutes or until the apples are tender. Put it under the broiler for a minute or two to crisp the top, if necessary. Remove the flan ring or the sides of the springform pan and allow the tart to cool a bit. Serve it warm or cool.

NOTE—*This recipe will make enough crust for a two-crust pie, but you will only need about half of the dough for the Apple Crisp Tart. The other half may be frozen for future use or used to make Cheese Sticks as follows: add 3–5 tablespoons of freshly grated Parmesan cheese and 1/4 teaspoon of salt to the leftover dough, work it in well and roll the dough between your palms to form little sticks about 2 inches long. Bake them at 375° F. on an ungreased cookie sheet for about 15 minutes.*

SUNDAY LUNCH

Omelette Provençale
Green Salad
French Bread

•

Prunes Crème Fraîche

OMELETTE PROVENÇALE

butter
1 large onion, diced
about 1 cup cooked potatoes, diced
about 1 cup Zucchini Salad, p. 184
tomato paste
salt and freshly ground pepper

12 eggs, lightly beaten

Melt a generous amount of butter in a skillet, add the onions, potatoes and zucchini salad and cook them over medium heat until they are golden brown. Stir in a tablespoon or so of tomato paste and season well with salt and pepper. Cook for a few more minutes.

Make six individual omelettes, using ½ cup of filling for each, or one large omelette if you prefer.

This omelette filling, without the tomato paste, makes a delicious Zucchini Hash to be served with poached or fried eggs.

GREEN SALAD

Use several kinds of crisp, fresh lettuce in this salad. Separate the leaves and wash them in cold water. Shake them well and dry them with paper or terry towels. Tear them into smallish pieces and toss them in this light dressing:

4 tablespoons olive oil
2 tablespoons lemon juice   } beaten together
1 small clove garlic, minced } with a fork
  salt and freshly ground pepper

PRUNES CRÈME FRAÎCHE

Your first taste of this creamy confection will be a deliciously tart surprise.

1 box (1 pound) dried pitted prunes
1 cup crème fraîche

coarse brown sugar (optional)

Put the prunes in a small bowl, cover them with boiling water and let them stand for about 30 minutes, until they are softened but still chewy. Drain them and cut them into small pieces.

Just before dinner, fold the prunes into the *crème fraîche*.

Serve small portions. Sprinkle with coarse brown sugar, if you wish.

CRÈME FRAÎCHE

Crème fraîche, a homemade sour cream, is an excellent accompaniment to many fruits and will keep for several weeks in the refrigerator.

Make it by stirring 1 teaspoon of buttermilk into one cup of heavy sweet cream (*see note*). Put the mixture in a jar, cover it, and allow it to stand in a warm place for 24 hours or until it is thickened. Refrigerate.

NOTE—*Double this recipe if you are making both Hot Bananas, p. 184, and Prunes Crème Fraîche.*

INDEX

Index

Index